FOCUS
Patterns for Christian Living

by
Dr. Henry Alloway

Harrison House
Tulsa, OK

15 14 13 12 11 10   9 8 7 6 5 4 3 2 1

Focus
ISBN 10: 1-60683-017-1
ISBN 13: 1-978-60683-017-8
Copyright © 2010 by Henry Alloway
1912 Ed Kharbat Dr.
Conroe, TX 77301

Published by Harrison House Publishers
P.O. Box 35035
Tulsa, Oklahoma 74153
www.harrisonhouse.com

CONTENTS

(The last chapter reveals what happened in the artist to cause him to paint pictures like the one on the cover)

FOREWORD

The commonplace experiences of life can become stale and stagnant. Frustrations can mount. Life can become drudgery. Relationships can fall apart. One can become unhappy with one's job. Joy departs. Meaning and purpose seem to fall by the wayside. One's children never seem to live up to one's standards or one's ambitions. The neighbors don't care for anyone except themselves. I have decided to just leave them alone; life is too complicated!

If any or all of the above mentioned conditions have previously or now exist in your life, then ask yourself WHY? Could it be that you have focused on the negative and lost sight of the positive? There is an old tune, made famous by Bing Crosby, which many of you have never heard. It says:

"Accentuate the positive, eliminate the negative, and don't mess with Mr. In-Between."

Why not make the positive the essence of your new lifestyle? Maybe all you need is the right kind of insight, revelation, and proper coaching in order to learn how to let your <u>inner man come alive</u> and begin to <u>blossom like a rose</u>.

Dr. Henry Alloway, (a retired Methodist minister and school teacher) and Dr. Roger Birkman (chairman of the board at BIRKMAN INTERNATIONAL, INC.) have combined their talents, skills, insights, biblical revelation, and personal experiences in an informative, interesting and challenging group dynamic format known as DISCOVERY GROUPS through the ministry of THE CHRISTIAN FAMILY INSTITUTE. The name Discovery Groups was given to Dr. Birkman by Rev. Rederick Marsh, an associate minister of his home church, The Methodist Church of Houston, Texas.

Discover yourself (your positive talents—insight), discover God (revelation—the Bible), discover your neighbor (wife, children, boss, etc.), and through this amazing discovery process begin to accentuate the positive; it pays!

This very practical book *FOCUS*, written by Dr. Henry Alloway is a means of helping (coaching) participants to better understand and apply the valuable insights gained through the use of THE BIRKMAN METHOD®, an interview questionnaire each participant fills out. It is a most valuable tool in interpreting accurate insight for the person who desires to accentuate the positive. Dr. Birkman's book *TRUE COLORS* is also a most meaningful amplification of the insights gained through the questionnaire, another "must" for your library. These two books complement each other.

As you begin to focus on the positive (talents), you will see how quickly you will be able to eliminate the negative (or turn it into a positive). Your life will take on a new dimension. Your frustrations will be turned into faith (positive), the joy of living will return...and the presence of the Lord will be our reward!

Joy returns! It's catching! It's wonderful! It's life lived everyday in the commonplace with uncommon power and praise. Stay focused on the Light (insight—revelation), and the Light will shine forth from you as the <u>light of the world</u> where you are, and you will experience a <u>new beginning</u>.

President Gerald Easterly
Talent Sharing, Inc.

PREFACE

A concept easily understood in our society is the concept of focus. Until a microscope is in clear focus, the subject of interest cannot be seen clearly. In our world we have made enough progress that we have developed automatic focus for many such things as cameras, video equipment, and other technological advancements. Focus is clearly understood as an important feature in the proper functional operation of equipment used to bring about clear images.

In a world that has developed so much technology for the purpose of bringing about clear images, we seem to be woefully lacking in technology that enables us to focus on inner problems and develop solutions that would be gratifying to us an individuals. It is not just the alcoholics, the drug abusers, the adulterers, the criminals, the prejudiced, and the homeless that need help. Every person lives in a fragile world that can be shattered in a moment of time. We need to have adequate preparation for anything that comes along. What possibly could be the answer to this dilemma?

I heard a story one time about a father who gave his young son a picture puzzle with the world on one side. The father knew that the little boy's knowledge of geography would not allow him to place the pieces there except by the laborious task of fitting piece to piece until it was completed. To his amazement, the boy finished the puzzle very quickly. Questioned by his father as to how he finished so quickly, the boy replied, "Father, a picture of Jesus was on the other side of the puzzle, when I put him together the world was right too."

This story represents to me a truth in the fact that Jesus should be the focal point for every human being. I am sure that many people would disagree, but when their world literally crumbles beneath their feet, if they can but focus on Jesus, He can help them put their world back together. Not any of us could possibly achieve what Jesus achieved, and we are not even supposed to strive for that achievement. We are to strive to be the best we can be in a world that needs a total contribution to life. Jesus can help us reach our greatest potential. It is not too late—some of the future is in our hands.

How do you focus on Jesus in a complex world? There are many people who seek Him by attending churches with many different doctrines. Some of these people find a deeply satisfying relationship with Him that brings a deep abiding strength to their lives. These people go about freely contributing good in the world about them. You will find them fulfilling what Jesus said when he was speaking of judgment. "I was hungry and you fed me." "I was thirsty and you gave me a drink." "I was naked and you clothed me", etc. Even though this occurs, many people attend church and do not come to this satisfying relationship with Jesus the Christ. Many give up going to church because it is not answering their needs. A statement I heard one time was "The church is too busy answering questions nobody is asking." If that is true, no wonder many people have given up on the church. Regardless of what is right or wrong with the Christian church, the need still exists for people to have a living, vital relationship with the Lord Jesus Christ so that their worlds can be brought into proper focus.

The subtitle *Patterns for Christian Living* is important to understand. A pattern is not the real thing, it is only designed to help you know how to develop the real thing. Jesus' description of a house built on a rock and a house built on the sand in Matthew 7 helps us to know that we should consider the foundation of our life. Jesus is the rock of our salvation. Sand is building on things that will not stand the test of eternity. The more you come to know Jesus Christ in this life, the more solid will be the foundation of your life.

It is to that end that this book is written, to help you to focus on the One that can add life to your living, hope for your hopelessness, joy for your sorrow, and peace in place of your fear. May God bless you as you read, and may Jesus come alive in your heart.

FOCUS ON COMMITMENT

O ne of Jesus' statements was "The light of the body is the eye: if therefore thine eye be single, thy whole body shall be full of light" (Matt. 6:22). When you ponder this scripture, you see that just before this Jesus said, "For where your treasure is, there will your heart be also" (Matt. 6:21). In verse 24, He says, "No man can serve two masters for either he will hate the one and love the other, or else he will hold to the one and despise the other. Ye cannot serve God and mammon."

Jesus lays down a very strong principle here that is like the first commandment given through Moses in Exodus 20 when He said, "Thou shalt have no other gods before me." This indeed can sound selfish of God for anyone who has not learned to trust Him, but for who have embraced this truth, they have learned that God is so insistent because He wants to bless them; He wants to bring to them the deepest desires of their hearts. God can do more for you than you think when you have a single eye.

A number of years ago, I had the privilege of teaching sixth graders in the public school in Daingerfield, Texas. It was a class 2-A school in a state that at that time classified schools through 4-A. I taught math and science several periods of the day, and I had a forty-five minute period used for preparation. The sixth graders had recess for that period. I thought it would be a good idea for me to take the sixth grade boys at that time and develop an intramural program with them. I chose team captains and had them choose teams, and through the year we played touch football, basketball, track and then softball. I did this for four years, and I saw a lot of good athletes develop.

In the third year, after we had completed our round-robin schedule in basketball and crowned our champions, I called those boys together and talked with them. I said, "Fellows, I believe there is enough talent and ability in this grade that if you would commit yourself to these three things, you could be state champions by the time you are seniors. If you will stick together, keep good attitudes, and get your work done in the classroom, you could do it." I went on to tell them that wherever I was when they got to the state tournament, I would try to come and see them play.

The next year after basketball was completed there was one boy that was an excellent floor leader, a great competitor, and a super ball handler. I called him aside and told him what I had told the group the year before him. I told him that I believed that he was needed as the point guard on that team.

I moved about 200 miles from Daingerfield the next year. Slowly, memories began to fade as several years passed by. Then one night as I was relaxing at home, the phone rang. I was greeted by a friendly voice that I recognized from years past. It was the father of the boy that I had spoken to about being the point guard. He said, "Mr. Alloway, do you remember what you told these boys when they were in sixth grade?" I knew what he was talking about and I told him so. He said, "They want me to let you know that they are going to the state tournament, and they would like for you to be there to see them play."

I made arrangements to be there—what a tremendous accomplishment for a group of young boys. They had set a goal—could they accomplish what they had set out to do as sixth graders?

When I arrived at the state tournament, I had decided not to try to see the boys before the game. I didn't want to break their concentration. I wanted them to be fully ready to meet another good team.

After finding our seats, my son and I went to get sodas for our family. I didn't realize that we would have to walk by the dressing room in Old Gregory Gym on the campus of the University of Texas. The coach was standing outside the dressing room and he saw me. "Mr. Alloway," he said, and I thought I saw a tear, "you started these boys out, didn't you? Why don't you go in to the dressing room and see them?"

I told him that I hadn't wanted to break their concentration, but I said, "You are the coach and I'll do whatever you think is best." He thought it over for a minute and then said, "I believe it would be a good thing for you to go in and see them."

I went into the dressing room and congratulated them for being in the state tournament. I started to leave when of the boys spoke to me and said, "Mr. Alloway, would you say a prayer for us?"

"Certainly!" I replied. Then before my eyes, every boy got down on his knees before God. I prayed a simple prayer and left the dressing room.

They literally demolished a very good opponent in their first game. It was only close at the beginning. Yes, they were a very good team. They played well. The team that they beat won state the next three years in a row.

Their opponent for the finals was another very good team. Coaches that we talked with told us that although Daingerfield had a very good team, they didn't think their chances were very good for beating Borger in the finals. They thought perhaps Borger was the best team in the state in all classes. Their concept seemed to be that even though Daingerfield had a very good team, they simply could not beat Borger.

We came the next day for the finals. We had taken our place in the stands when all of the sudden they announced my name over the public address system and asked me to come to the scoring table for a message. Being a minister, I imagined it was an emergency from home regarding one of my parishioners. Before I reached the scoring table, the assistant coach met me and told me that the boys wanted me to come to the dressing room.

As I walked into the dressing room, I reminded the boys of what I had told them as sixth graders—that if they stuck together, kept good attitudes, and made their grades, I didn't see any reason why they couldn't be state champions by the time they were seniors. I told them that they had done all those things, and I wanted them to know that they were already champions because they had paid the price. They had done what champions have to do. I told them it didn't matter how the game turned out; they were already champions because they had developed the attitude of champions.

Then I said, "One more thing, fellows. When this season started, there were over 200 teams in your division that wanted to be state champions. Now only two teams have that opportunity, and you are one of them." The last thing I said was "Fellows, I don't believe any group of boys deserves to be champions more than you do. Just go out there, relax, and do your best."

The game was something else—one of the most exciting games one would ever hope to see. It was nip and tuck—tooth and toenail—all the way. Never more than 3 or 4 points separated the two teams. Someone had to win. Someone had to lose. Two valiant foes gave 100 percent effort. What a game! When it was all over I had to go to the same dressing room to congratulate the state champions. These boys had done what critics said could not be done. They had won when expected to lose. They truly were champions.

Some members of that team were given college scholarships. Three of them eventually played professional football. They had learned what it takes to be a champion.

Another memory that sparkles for me was what happened in Daingerfield while I was there. I was the radio announcer for a football team that won the state championship. As the announcer, I had the privilege to be in the dressing room right after the game so I could do interviews. They had just won the championship by a score of 7-6 over a team that had won two successive state championships and 39 straight games without a loss.

You can imagine the joy and excitement in the dressing room. The noise was beyond description, and then the coach got their attention and everything was very quiet. It was just before Christmas as playoffs in Texas take several weeks. The coach said, "Boys, the good Lord has been with us for nineteen weeks and He has given us the best Christmas gift that a group of boys could ever want—a state championship. Let's have a prayer and then greet our friends." The Amen was lost in the wild shouts of joy as the prayer ended.

What do these stories have in common? Even though they were groups of people they had a common purpose, a single eye. Jesus said, "When two agree as touching anything in my name, I will do it" (Matt. 18:19). Many times it is difficult for a person to develop a single eye. When that single eye is developed by a person, it allows them to be very creative. When two or more people can unite in a common purpose, even greater things can be accomplished. Jesus said, "When two or three are gathered together in my name, I am there in their midst" (Matt. 18:20).

God indeed has a purpose for your life. No one else can fill it for you. You can do it if you will. God is your ally to help you, if you will let Him. The real focus for our lives starts here with a commitment to do the will of God and to have no other gods before us. It is so simple that many people trip over its simplicity.

COMMITMENT
Questions to Think About

1. What is the greatest commitment of my life?

2. Is that commitment producing all that I think it should produce for the satisfaction of my life?

3. What kind of commitments have I made with other people?

4. Am I fulfilling my part in the commitments that I have made?

5. If I have made any commitments that I cannot keep or should not keep, how can I resolve them?

6. If I could tell the story about my life with God, what would I tell?

Focus

FOCUS ON FORGIVENESS

In the Bible we read, "All have sinned and have fallen short of the glory of God" (Romans 3:23). In the Lord's Prayer we pray, "Forgive us our trespasses as we forgive those who trespass against us" (Matt. 6:12). It further says in Matthew 6:14-15, "If you forgive, your Heavenly Father will forgive you, but if you do not forgive then you will not be forgiven." Somewhere in those passages we should be able to figure out that God fully intends for us to be forgiving. What we may not have figured out is the kind of blessings we are missing when we fail to forgive.

When I was a pastor at St. John's United Methodist Church in Port Arthur, Texas, a curious thing happened. My lay leader learned that I had available to me, The Birkman Method®, a questionnaire that would enable people to focus on different aspects of their personality. He wanted me to bring it to our church as he was teaching a leadership course, and he wanted them to take it and learn from its concepts. The problem for me was that in order to use it, I had to fill it in and get the results for myself. That seemed a bit scary to me. I was not sure that I wanted to know that much about my inner life. I suppose I was afraid of the unknown; afraid that this would reveal something terrible about me.

Focus

With the gentle pressure applied by my lay leader, I got the results, talked with Dr. Birkman about the results, and learned how to interpret the information to our people. The leadership group then filled in the questionnaire, and I talked with them about what it revealed about their strengths, their needs, and their weaknesses. As news spread from that group to others in the church, within six months I had more than seventy-five people come to me to fill it in and talk with me about the results. My personal counseling load became so heavy that I had to begin meeting with people in groups. Before long, I had forty-eight different people meeting with me once a week in four different groups. People were eager to find answers for long lasting and difficult problems. Some found far more than what they thought they would find when they began.

One man in particular had one of the most unique experiences I have ever encountered. He was a member of our church but not very regular in his attendance—a fine man with a good family but not one to be greatly concerned about church attendance. I announced in our church newsletter that I was going to start one of these groups, and I was quite surprised when he showed up at the appointed time and place.

I explained to them the first night about what we would do as a group. We would use The Birkman Method® for insight. We would use the book *Prayer Can Change Your Life* by Parker and St. Johns for inspiration. We would use the four Gospels—the teachings of Jesus—for correction. Each group meeting would last 1½ hours. We would begin with prayer and end with prayer, but the rest of the time would be spent in sharing our scores and the understanding of what they meant for each of us. In this process we were able to see the relevance of Scripture and Its guidance for us in relationship to life. I also told them that although the sessions would last 1½ hours that I would be available after each session for any individual that wanted to stay after the meeting to talk with me.

We had met for several weeks. The groups had become quite well adjusted to one another. They were able to communicate pretty well by that time. In the group meeting that night, there was a discussion about forgiveness. One man seemed to have quite a bit of trouble with the concept of forgiveness; he seemed to think that there were some justifiable reasons for unforgiveness. We struggled as a group trying to deal with this.

When the group concluded, the man stayed to visit with me. I kept giving him the things that Jesus said, "Forgive unto seventy times seven" (Matt. 18:22), "Forgive and you will be forgiven" (Luke 6:37), and any other Scriptures that I could use to help him see that forgiveness was vital for our life. He did not tell the group or me what caused his problem with forgiveness, but it was obvious that he had a real hang-up with forgiveness.

The group meeting had ended at 9:00 p.m. It was after midnight when he left my house, but by the grace of God, he had become convinced that forgiveness was absolutely necessary. When he came back to our group meeting, he shared a story with all of us that was heartwarming, exhilarating, inspirational and deeply moving.

He started out by telling us about his important job with the Texaco refinery in Port Arthur. He was in charge of a unit that could be dangerous, and he was in charge of a number of men. He told about how he had developed a skin condition on his feet that seemed to defy healing. He had gone to six different medical doctors including several skin specialists. All they could do was of no avail, his feet would not heal.

He then told us about the night that he had become thoroughly convinced that he must forgive. Then he told us about his problem. His mother and father owned a large rice farm. He lived on one side of them, and his brother lived on the other side of them. They both helped their dad with the farming. When the mother and father died, they left everything they had to his brother. He literally hated them for it.

I need to stop here and say what a horrible thing it is to harbor unforgiveness. For anyone who has unforgiveness, it means that they have been hurt somehow, some way, at some time or another. It is bad enough that you have been hurt, but if you are harboring unforgiveness, you are allowing that person to hurt you in a far deeper way. Your spirit is being oppressed by the unforgiveness. It sometimes takes a heavy toll even on the physical body. Do not let unforgiveness destroy you.

Back to this man's story. He went on to say that he left my house convinced of what he had to do: he knew that he must forgive his father and mother. He didn't know how to go about it—his mother and father were dead—so he decided to get on his knees before God, and he said this prayer: "My heavenly Father, I come to You tonight to ask You to forgive me for having unforgiveness in my heart toward my father and mother.

I would like for them to know that I forgive them, but I cannot go to them but You can. I ask You to let them know that I have forgiven them".

He told us then that a warm sensation began to occur in his physical body. It started in his head and went all through his body. The thing that amazed him and us the most was that his feet were instantaneously healed. He never had any more problems with them.

I don't understand what happened, but I do know the facts in this case. In my mind, I am quite sure that forgiveness made a great difference in this man's life.

FORGIVENESS
Questions to Think About

1. Have I ever recognized any wrongdoing in my life?

2. If the answer to number one is yes, did I feel the need for someone to forgive me?

3. If the answer to number one is no, am I able to face the fact that I am not perfect in every respect?

4. Am I willing to forgive people for wrong things they have done to me?

5. If I am having problems with forgiveness, who can I talk with about the situation?

6. Am I willing to open my heart to God, to share with Him the deep feelings of unforgiveness that I have harbored?

7. Can I truly forgive and not wish any negative thing to happen to those I forgive?

FOCUS ON
AUTHORITY

Very early in a child's life they begin dealing with authority. Their will to do something is met by an older person who wills something else. How the problem is handled is important for both of them.

Let's consider a hypothetical situation where a child is perhaps one-year old and persists in running out into the street. You might talk to the child and tell him not to do it. Some children might respond well to that expression of concern and might not ever run into the street again. How fortunate!

Another child might continue to run into the street even after being told not to do so. You might even try explaining the physical nature of the possibility that exists—a 3,000 pound automobile hits your 30 pound body at 30 miles an hour; it's wheels roll over your body, and you would be crushed to death by force of the impact. Little children could not understand the complexities of that explanation. They might continue to run into the street. You still have the responsibility for their safety, so what do you do?

Getting someone to respond properly to authority is not always easy. In the case of a little child, one might finally have to apply pain to the seat of their pants. They have not been able to comprehend the gentle command or the extended explanation, but perhaps they could understand that every time they went in to the street, it brought pain to the seat of their pants—and in order to stop the pain, they must quit going into the street.

This is a simple analogy of what happens every day in our society. People struggle with authority. Those who learn to adjust to the demands of authority seem to get along well. Those who have problems with it keep getting into more and more difficulty. Perhaps a better understanding of authority and our response to it would help all of us to avoid the pain that is necessary when we keep having trouble with authority.

Besides being a minister, I have taught for twenty-three years in the public schools of Texas. Many young people have a very favorable response to authority—they learn to adjust and bring themselves into compliance with the demands of that authority. Some young people seem to have a great many problems when it comes to acceptance of most authority.

Good teachers try to find a way to reach those students and find some approach that is workable for that student. The child who continuously has problems generally spends much time in the office, in detention, and even suspended. This is a major problem for the schools of America.

For seven years, I went as a volunteer chaplain to the Walls unit of the Texas Prison in Huntsville, Texas. I spoke in the prison chapel to about 300 inmates every Sunday afternoon. I met with a group of about thirty inmates on Saturday afternoons in the prison library. I became very well acquainted with a number of prisoners. I never did meet with one that planned to be in prison. I became aware of the fact that what takes people to prison is their difficulty in relating to authority.

Authority can come to us in many different ways, and we have to recognize that all authority is not good. We can start with a child in an abusive home situation, and see it continue with teachers who sometimes smile upon some children and frown upon others. (Having been there I know how easy it is to like some children and how difficult it is to like others—nevertheless it is so important—teachers need to find something they can like in every student.) The pattern continues in job situations where conflicts arise, tempers flare, and employment is terminated. The law comes to us in many different ways. All of us have broken laws to some extent, but the problems arise when you lose all respect for the law and deliberately break it time and time again. This is where incarceration begins and freedom ends. It is not a very pretty picture.

Authority can be issued in different ways. It can be given as a direct command from someone who has authority over you. It may come as a suggestion with the realization that you are expected to respond appropriately. When I was in seminary, I worked at Chance-Vaught Aircraft in Grand Prairie, Texas. We were given a percentage on what was expected of us each night. This became an authority situation because we were evaluated as an assembly line worker in terms of percentage output. As a teacher in Texas, the state legislature enacted legislation in which our superiors would evaluate our performance as a teacher in the classroom based on a number of different criteria. Some of these were classroom management, discipline, learning atmosphere, attitude toward students, etc. We were aware that even though supervisors were committed to objectivity, there was a great deal of subjectivity in the process. This boiled down to the fact that evaluation systems also represent a system of authority. Success with the authority represented has something to do with job security. A certain amount of stress is involved with everyone, but some people feel the effects of that stress more than others, and it seems to largely relate to how they get along with their supervisors.

In our understanding of The Birkman Method®, we have recognized that some people have considerably different inner needs as they relate to authority. Some people may find their needs cutting across the sets of needs that I mention, whereas some people might recognize their needs pretty well expressed by one example or the other.

To use a hypothetical situation, let's take John Doe. He might have this set of needs as outlined in some of the Birkman literature. He needs:

A) carefully defined and enforced boundaries,

B) superiors and associates who are firm and forceful,

C) opportunities to discuss, debate, and argue,

D) authoritative and direct supervision, and

E) work situations which satisfy his need to direct others.

Let's now consider John Q. Public whose inner needs differ from J.D. His needs might include:

A) clearly defined, formally delegated authority,

B) a high degree of self-determined activities,

C) agreeable and pleasant relationships,

D) encouragement to express real feelings and views, and

E) suggestions and persuasion rather than direct orders.

Should your needs compare with those of John Doe, but you are working in a situation where the authority structure is like that expressed in the analogy by John Q. Public, at best you might feel a bit uncomfortable in that situation. On the other hand, if you are working in a situation which is structured by what meets your inner needs for authority, you would feel much better.

If you have any problem with the authority structures in your life, you are probably wondering, "What can I do to resolve this problem in my life?" Believing that God's Word, the Bible, has some things to say to us that could be helpful for us when we learn to apply it to our interpersonal needs, I would like to make some suggestions. For those who need direct commands, I would say, "Thus saith the Lord!"

The Apostle Paul admonishes us in 1 Timothy 2:1-3, "I exhort, therefore, that, first of all, supplications, prayers, intercessions, and giving of thanks, be made for all men; for kings and for all that are in authority, that we may lead a quiet and peaceable life in all godliness and honesty. For this is good and acceptable in the sight of God our Saviour."

I hear Paul saying that what is good in the sight of God our Savior is that we pray for all people intently, especially world leaders and for all of those in authority. Have you ever tried praying for those in authority over you? I believe that your support and prayers for them can pay real dividends for you.

Years ago I was in a school situation where the new principal was not well-liked or appreciated by the teachers. I tried to get along with everyone, but I could not join into their negative conversations about our boss. I prayed for him and for them knowing that we needed a healthy respect for authority. As time passed, I would go into the teacher's lounge and hear them saying things about the principal, but knowing how I felt, they quickly silenced their conversation. It seemed to me that I was becoming more and more unpopular with the faculty as I quietly stood behind the authority of the principal. At the end of the school year that principal retired and to my amazement the faculty requested that I become the principal. I appreciated the confidence expressed in me, even though I did not have proper certification for the job.

Through the years I have made a point of praying for all of the authorities in my life. I believe that God is the prime authority and that he has set authority in place in this world. I believe that authority figures who continually use their authority properly will be exalted. I believe that authority structures that are unsound shall fall away.

I have had people tell me that when they started praying for their boss in a situation that was difficult for them that they began to see some changes. In some cases the person praying was transferred, in other cases the boss was transferred, and in some cases the relationship between the boss and them greatly improved.

I could give you a good many Scriptures regarding your relationship with authority, but all of them would be negligible unless you took them to heart. If you wish to look further, you can use a concordance and look up Scripture after Scripture on authority. The final analysis, however, with what will happen in your future regarding authority depends on your attitude toward the authority you have in your life.

AUTHORITY
Questions to Think About

1. What do I recognize as the prime authority in my life?

2. How would I describe my childhood, relating to those in authority over me?

3. Do I now have respect for those who are in authority over me?

4. Am I afraid of those in authority over me? How might this relate to childhood memories?

5. What are my places of authority in this world?

6. Am I making good use of the authority given me?

7. Is there anything that I can do to improve my relationship with authority?

FOCUS ON MARRIAGE

All across the world people take the vows of marriage. In different cultures and religions the vows may differ, but I suppose that all of them have some things in common—two people from diverse backgrounds agreeing to live together with a public agreement "to love and to cherish, for better, for worse, for richer, for poorer, until death." That is a pretty large commitment. Many marriages have failed and are failing because people are not able to work through the problems they face within their marriage.

The Birkman Method® plus a commitment to the Lord Jesus Christ have been very important ingredients in the fifty-nine years of successful marriage for my wife and me. I suppose we could have made it without The Birkman Method®, but The Birkman Method® has really made a difference in many respects.

What we have learned in years of using The Birkman Method® as a counseling tool is that most marriages occur when the people involved have emotional and psychological responses to life that have a good many similarities. Where these similarities occur, they may not agree, but they can understand the emotional responses of their mates. The problems of deeper significance are in areas where they are greatly different and do not understand the opposite emotional response. Let me try to help you understand some of what I am talking about.

One couple we worked with loved one another very much, but they were having some intense problems. An understanding of their emotional responses in one area of their personalities helped both of them considerably. The man had a great deal of physical energy, and he was an action-oriented person. On the other hand, the wife had very little physical energy and was a reflective-oriented person. The marriage was just about to fold. The man was operating with the idea that everyone was like he was, except that some of them were lazy. He would get up at 4:00 A.M., go to the marsh to run his mink traps, and be at work at 7:00 A.M. as a supervisor of men. He would drive them all day, expecting them to have the same energy and action orientation that he had. After work he would return to the marsh and set his traps for the night. He could not understand his wife's need to read and to spend time in quiet reflection. In short, he was about to drive his wife and the men under his supervision into emotional, if not physical, collapse.

In the group relationship, he began to realize the differences in people and the variance of their emotional needs. It made a great difference in him. The men at work were grateful and the work relationship improved immensely. His wife was able to survive, and their marriage was happier than ever before.

My wife and I saw differences in our response to life that put both of us under pressure. Until we understood what those differences were, she wondered what was wrong with me, and I wondered what was wrong with her. The truth is that both of us were all right, but we had different emotional needs in some areas of our lives.

One major difference was that my wife needed a great sense of predictability in life. I had very little need for it. An example of the kind of problems produced was that I might be in my study and see the need to go for consultation with Dr. Birkman about a counseling problem. I would call his office, 100 miles away, and find out if I could see him in a couple of hours. I would walk across the street to tell my wife, at home, that I would be leaving in five minutes to go to Dr. Birkman's office. She wouldn't say anything, but the look on her face would indicate, "What's the matter with you, Henry? A trip like that needs to be planned in advance."

That kind of response on her part would trigger another emotional conflict between us. She always felt that if she didn't say anything, the problem would go away, but my emotional need was to talk about anything and everything until it was resolved. Consequently she was the type that would puff up and I was the type that would blow up.

Even problems like this can be resolved when both parties are committed to do the will of God. Understanding enables us to recognize the other's needs and try to help them to have their needs met. The Golden Rule is "Do unto others as you would have others do unto you" (Matt. 7:12). When I am trying to help my wife have her needs met, my own life will be blessed immeasurably.

My wife's predictability also includes the feeling that there is a place for everything, and everything should be in its place.

I appreciate the clean and orderly house my wife keeps, but I still have the problem of taking something and throwing it in the corner. To me, it's in its place. Thank God for a wife with much patience. She hasn't given up on me yet.

Marriage is a sacred covenant, and no one has more interest in its success than God himself. He instituted the home before He did the church. He wants the home to survive the many perils it faces in today's world. If you are having difficulty in your home, look for your answers. God will help you.

When I marry a couple, I ask for some insurance on their marriage. I ask them to promise me that if they ever have a problem that seems too difficult for them to work out between them, they will come back to me, a minister in whom they have confidence, or a competent marriage counselor to try to work through their problems. Only God knows the effect of that insurance.

"For better, for worse" is one of the vows. The *better* is the way you feel when you are married, the honeymoon, and many happy times thereafter. The *worse* comes about in the little failures, the temper tantrums, the depression, the lack of meaningful communication, and millions of other things that come up in individual marriages. Marriage can only survive when people realize that everyone makes mistakes. Forgive and be forgiven. God will help you.

I heard a sermon one time on the four anchors of the home. The preacher suggested the anchors as love, laughter, loyalty, and Lord. The love he was talking about was agape love in which people are concerned about having the needs met of people around them. Laughter is so important, not that we laugh at people but we laugh together. It breaks the tension, eases the strain, clears that air, and helps a lot. Loyalty doesn't usually make headlines. You find loyalty in the golden wedding section of the Sunday newspaper. For any family to begin marriage without God's blessing and help is like a ship leaving port without a rudder. We need God's help in marriage.

Marriage is beautiful and it is difficult. The more we can understand the emotional needs of our mate, the greater the chance of the survival of our marriage. Understanding by itself cannot get the job done. It takes commitment to agape love along with that understanding to bring about good results. This simply means that we must understand our mate's needs and work toward the supply of that need. Even if we fail, our effort should be strong enough that our mate knows that we really care. Marriage should be a loving, caring, sharing relationship that eventually brings about the best in both people.

Don't give up on your marriage; do everything in your power to make it work. There are so many positives that good marriages can produce—the children, the grandchildren, the great grandchildren and the many blessings that come in a caring family relationship. It is worth the effort, and God is your greatest ally.

MARRIAGE
Questions to Think About

If I am unmarried:

1. What qualities do I need to bring to the marriage altar?

2. When considering marriage, do I communicate well in social, financial, and spiritual realms?

3. What kind of adjustments will be made between my current life and married life?

4. Do I consider marriage as a lifetime contract?

If I am married:

1. Do I recognize some differences between my mate and me?

2. Are these differences making a negative difference in our relationship?

3. If differences occur, can we agree on seeking outside help?

4. What good things can happen through a marriage where each partner tries hard to make that relationship work?

FOCUS ON THE FUNCTIONAL FAMILY

In the past few years, you have probably read and heard many things about the dysfunctional family. A juvenile does something contrary to the law. It is said that he came from a dysfunctional family. A young adult commits a heinous crime, and it is argued in court that he is the product of a dysfunctional family. Many situations as these are attributed to the dysfunctional family: school problems with misbehavior, welfare cases where support is given, runaways, and drug and alcohol addiction. I have no argument with all of that reasoning even though good families sometimes have disappointing failures.

I do recognize that with all of the talk about the dysfunctional family, we do not see a lot of printed material about the functional family. If I do not want my family to be a dysfunctional family, how can I produce a functional family? I believe that the Word of God can guide us to a thorough understanding of what is needed in a functional family. I would like to share my understanding of what it takes to develop a functional family.

In a functional family there is a need for authority. Recognizing that all authority is not good, it is still important that we understand the need and the importance of authority in the home.

Focus

I remember an old story about a discussion between two people about why they couldn't get along. One of them used the example about a team of horses and how they pulled together when the other one said, "Yes, but they only have one tongue between them." To push that a little further than it truly allows, I would like to say that in a home it is important to be unified around a central authority. It gives a sense of comfort to have someone leading the way, setting the boundaries, giving instruction, supporting good decisions, discussing parameters, and the consequences of good and bad behavior. If there is someone in the home that can provide that kind of leadership, the whole world will profit from it.

We need to consider several things from the Bible that should give us some help in understanding how a functional family should relate. The first Scripture I would use is in 1 Corinthians 11:11-12. I like the way it is given in *The Living Bible*. "But remember that in God's plan men and women need each other. For although the first woman came out of man, all men have been from women ever since, and both men and women come from God their Creator."

For anyone who has trouble with that concept, you must realize that every philosophy of life has a basic foundation. Whatever philosophy you accept, you must know that in the foundation of that philosophy is a leap of faith. No man has all knowledge in himself. For those who have problems accepting God and His only begotten Son, Jesus Christ, there is a poem written by an unknown poet that says:

Focus on The Functional Family

A lot of people say they don't believe in God.

They don't believe in anything unless they can see it.

Look, friend, you can't see the electricity

In that high tension wire up yonder,

But I dare you to touch it.

No, you can't see the electricity,

But you can see the light.

God's Word provides light for all of those who have a heart to listen to it. Men and women need one another. That is the basis of the family. The human family has developed the most complex association of relationships in the whole universe. Many other varieties of living creatures have family relationships but none more complex than the human family. If the human family is going to function properly, they are going to need to follow the basic guidelines of the Creator. The first concept is that men and women need one another. If family involved only a sexual relationship and that was the end of the need, family life would never develop.

Men and women need one another in every area of life. They become stabilizing forces for one another in the mystifying experiences of life. Their relationship can provide warmth and comfort and strength that both of them need. Two, united together, are much stronger than one individual by himself.

Compatibility in marriage is a key factor, not just in sexual activities, but stretching through all areas of life. Ideally that compatibility includes spiritual, emotional, social, intellectual, financial, and visionary ideas. Very few of us, if any, can boast of all of those factors working perfectly in our marriage, but we should have enough similarities to give that marriage hope. This to me is one of the greatest reasons why young people should wait for marriage to have sex.

Sexual acts outside marriage may produce instant satisfaction, but it can also be complicated with guilt feelings, possible cause of disease, and problem pregnancies. How many marriages have occurred simply because of unplanned pregnancies? When marriage occurs for that simple reason, you might expect some complex problems. Many times these marriages do work out because of the good relationship and because both parties give themselves to the success of that marriage and make whatever sacrifices need to be made to make it a working family.

In the large part, however, marriages and families have better chances with some basic understandings regarding the factors mentioned earlier. The more agreement that a man and woman can accomplish before their marriage should help them considerably after their marriage. The key factor in a good marriage is a good relationship between the man and the woman.

Communication between a husband and wife is perhaps the most important factor in their marriage. An old concept often declared is that when a married couple has a fight, (not physical) the best part is in making up. What is important about this is that some real communication has taken place. Even though a word has not been spoken, forgiveness has been given, and the couple is again able to work together to solve the problems of life.

Authority in the home, then, is tempered by the relationship of the husband and wife, but even in a good relationship, the authority of the father should be recognizable in a functional family. I am sure some people would argue with that concept, but Paul says in 1 Corinthians 11:3 in *The Living Bible*, "But there is one matter I want to remind you about: that a wife is responsible to her husband, her husband is responsible to Christ, and Christ is responsible to God."

In the broader concept of authority, the husband is not the lord over his household, but he is recognized by God as the authority in the home and is held responsible before God in the way he manifests that authority with his family. When I say that God stands behind the authority of the father, I am speaking of that authority that lives in respect unto the heavenly Father.

I remember a circumstance years ago when a young father came home from work around midnight. He was greeted at the door by a worried wife, because their little child had a very high fever. This man bore witness that he went in to see the child and felt great compassion for the child. He put his hand on the child's fevered brow and started praying for the child. To his amazement, the fever broke and the child quickly recovered.

In another instance that I relate fully in another book that I have written, *It All Began in Slate Valley*, published by Harrison House, I wrote about a father who was in prison. His child was desperately ill, and he couldn't go and see the child. He asked that I pray with him for the child. We prayed, God answered his prayer, and his child's health was restored.

I believe that God recognizes the authority of the husband and honors that authority when the man comes before him, respects him, and asks in simple faith for answers to his family's needs. The home becomes dysfunctional when a father refuses to respect the authority of God and take the authority God expects him to take. When a husband takes authority, it does not mean that he becomes a tyrant. Rather, he becomes the responsible person when the family has communicated, has recognized the problem, and has brought all of their resources together to face the problem; but then someone has to say what will be done. This becomes a part of the role of a good father in the functional home.

In Ephesians 5:25-28 TLB the husband is instructed, "And you husbands, show the same kid of love to your wives as Christ showed to the church when he died for her, to make her holy and clean, washed by baptism and God's word; so that he could give her to himself as a glorious church without a single spot or wrinkle, or any other blemish, being holy and without a single fault. That is how husbands should treat their wives, loving them as parts of themselves. For since a man and his wife are now one, a man is really doing himself a favor and loving himself when he loves his wife." This admonition for a husband to love his wife even as Christ loved the church and gave Himself for it shows the sacrificial nature of the husband and father.

In Paul's chapter on love, he says, "It's like this: when I was a child I spoke and thought and reasoned as a child does. But when I became a man my thoughts grew far beyond those of my childhood, and now I have put away those childish things"

Focus on The Functional Family

(I Corinthians 13:11 TLB). A husband's maturity should bring him to the place of sacrificial service to his wife and his children. He begins to make choices that will honor them, assert discipline that will enable them to be successful, provide wisdom that will help them emotionally in times of crisis, and provide for them the necessities of life. All of this and much more is required of a husband and father in a functional home.

In Ephesians 5:21-24 TLB, we read: "Honor Christ by submitting to each other. You wives must submit to your husband's leadership in the same way you submit to the Lord. For a husband is in charge of his wife in the same way Christ is in charge of his body the church. (He gave his very life to take care of it and be its Savior!) So you wives must willingly obey your husbands in everything, just as the church obeys Christ." This instruction to a wife, when followed, can be greatly helpful in a home.

A few years ago, a woman came to me in great distress. She and her husband were not getting along. She was a Christian and trying to be a good one. Her husband did not come to church and was not living a life of dedication to God. As the wife was telling me all about the problems in their marriage, she included the fact that often her husband would come in from work in the evening and he would want to have sex. She said that although she physically entered into a sexual relationship with him, it was more or less torture to her. She was not involved emotionally. She felt that she was only being used of her husband to provide him with sexual satisfaction. Their marriage had deteriorated almost to the breaking point.

I started talking with her about the Scripture, "Wives, submit yourselves unto your own husbands, as unto the Lord" (Ephesians 5:22). I explained to her the fact that sometimes it is very difficult for a wife to submit herself to her own husband. She lives with him every day. She probably sees a lot of good in him, but she also sees his faults that begin to drive her to distraction. How can she submit to a husband in whom she sees so many faults?

I helped her to see that she really needed help here that the Scripture says, "Be subject to your husband, AS UNTO THE LORD." I asked her, "Do you know of anything that is wrong with the Lord Jesus Christ?"

She said, "No," so I talked to her about the prerequisite for submission to a husband is submission to the Lord.

I said, "When he asks you to do anything; in your heart, you ask if it is all right with the Lord of your life, Jesus Christ. If it is all right with the Lord, then you should be able to submit to your husband."

This seemed to make sense to her as she was a devoted Christian. In a few weeks, the husband started coming to church. He soon was a born again Christian. About six months after the conversation with the wife, the husband came to me and thanked me for my counsel with his wife. It had made a great difference in their marriage, their home, and their family.

We need to recognize that our first loyalty is to the Lord, but when we operate under His supreme authority in our lives, He can bring all other things into proper alignment with Him. The fruit of a woman in subjection unto the Lord and to her husband in the home produces the qualities found in Proverbs 31:10-31. These are some of the qualities mentioned:

A)The heart of her husband doth safely trust in her.

B)She will do him good and not evil all the days of her life.

C)Strength and honor are her clothing; and she shall rejoice in time to come.

D)She opens her mouth with wisdom; and in her tongue is the law of kindness.

E)She looketh well to the ways of her household, and eateth not the bread of idleness.

As you read through the other verses, you find Scripture to support the working woman, but the climax comes in verse thirty, when the writer declares, "Favour is deceitful, and beauty is vain; but a woman that feareth the Lord, she shall be praised."

God has exalted women to a very high and wonderful place in the world. The home was the first institution set up by God on earth, and the woman is the hub of the home; everything revolves around her. She properly relates to her husband and the father of her children. She nourishes with her own body a newborn baby and cares for each child until they spring forth unto maturity. The place of a wife and mother in the home is equally important with the father if the home is to be a functional home.

Now we turn our attention to the children in a functional home. Ephesians 6:1-3 TLB emphatically states, "Children, obey your parents; this is the right thing to do because God has placed them in authority over you. Honor your father and mother. This is the first of God's Ten Commandments that ends with a promise. And this is the promise: that if you honor your father and mother, yours will be a long life, full of blessing." All of us like to be blessed, and this simply states what a child can do to obtain God's blessing for a long life filled with many different but wonderful experiences. The difficulty in obtaining the blessing is to bring yourself in subjection unto the parents. Again, children see the faults of the parents, and they need help in being able to respond to the authority they represent.

God gives parents an admonition that would help when parents can heed the advice found in Ephesians 6:4 TLB "And now a word to you parents. Don't keep on scolding and nagging your children, making them angry and resentful. Rather, bring them up with the loving discipline the Lord himself approves with suggestions and godly advice." When you are disciplining children, maybe you need to ask, "Am I doing this for my child's sake, or is it just to appease my anger for his failure?" Kids are going to fail just like adults fail—what they need is to know that they are loved even while they are being disciplined.

A father told one time about paddling his son, and after the paddling, he asked the son, "Do you know why I did this?"

The son replied, "Yes, I know, because you are bigger than I am."

Something was lost in the communication. Even so, children will not always understand the discipline, but discipline should be used to change their direction from something that is wrong to something that is right. Forms of discipline can vary greatly, but whatever it is, unless real love can shine through, it is difficult for the child to get the right answer.

So in the functional home, the key is love. If your home does not possess the love you need, it is not too late. It starts with Jesus and ends with Jesus. When families begin to look for and find a meaningful relationship with Jesus Christ, a dysfunctional home can be changed into a functional home. Life can be better than it has even been before—but also just like turning a light on and then turning it off—this can be done in a home. A constant everyday relationship with Jesus Christ is supremely important to the real success of any home.

To climax this chapter, an unknown poet declares the tragedy that often takes place but can be corrected when the human heart turns again to God.

"Does Jesus live at your house?" I heard a child once ask.
Her little brow was furrowed as she struggled with a task.
"He used to live at our house with Mamma and Daddy too.
But now, He's gone away somewhere, and I don't know what to do.
For Daddy is not the same today, and Mamma laughs no more,
They never bother much with me—They say I'm just a bore.
But it didn't used to be this way, with Jesus in our home;
For every night my daddy came, when all my curls were combed,
And helped me say my bedtime prayers.

And Mamma helped me too!

And then they smiled and tucked me in,

But now—They never do.

Could you tell me where Jesus is? For everything seems black;

We want Him in our home again, we want Him to come back.

And when He comes, we'll keep Him, for we truly need Him so.

If Jesus lives at your house, Oh, don't ever let Him go."

The child then turned and left me. While I pursued my way,

And thoughts of many home fires that could be bright today.

Does Jesus live at your house?

How much those words portend.

Yes, on that question's answer, Our hopes, our all, depend.

God wants to help you with your family. The journey of a thousand miles begins with the first step. May your home receive the blessing of God.

FUNCTIONAL FAMILY
Questions to Think About

1. How many members of my family will help me develop a functional family?

2. In what way can I help those who are presently unwilling to work toward a functional home?

3. Are there needs in my family that indicate a need for some outside help?

4. Is there good communication between parents and children?

5. What problems seem to be the most difficult? Some possibilities could be financial, spiritual, alcohol, drugs, social, etc.

6. What local agencies, government agencies, or churches might have help for our needs?

7. What good things can happen in my family as we develop a functional home?

Focus

FOCUS ON YOUR CHILDREN

Psalms 128 TLB, we read:

Blessings on all who reverence and trust the Lord on all who obey Him. Their reward shall be prosperity and happiness. Your wife will be contented in your home. And look at all those children! There they sit, around the dinner table as vigorous and healthy as young olive trees. That is God's reward to those who reverence and trust Him. May the Lord continually bless you with heaven's blessings as well as with human joys. May you live to enjoy your grandchildren! And may God bless Israel!

This great blessing of God is promised to those who trust the Lord and obey Him. Seeing healthy children is a great reward for those who really reverence God.

In this passage, it talks about sitting around the dinner table. Just how important can it be to have some time together as a family? Using simple arithmetic, if a family spent one hour a day together at the dinner table, or at breakfast, or whenever their schedules brought them together, it would make a great difference in the molding of their lives. If a child has an average of one hour a day with his parents for fifteen of his eighteen years, that would amount to 5,475 hours. A teacher who teaches your child for a full school year of 180 days for a possible 7 hours a day would only have your child for 1,260 hours. If you went to church every Sunday for 15 years of a child's first 18 years, and they received 3 hours of instruction every week, that would be 2,340 hours of instruction. This should help you to recognize that the prime source of communication for children comes in the home.

How much quality is built into the communication between parents and other siblings in the home is somewhat dependent on the management of your home. In modern society, television plays such an important role because so much time is spent watching whatever is produced, rather than using disciplinary guidelines regarding programs to watch. How many homes have their communication cut to a minimum because of their interest in television? Should my children be raised by whatever is on television? Parental management of time at home is the only hope for real communication within the home.

The way people communicate will differ in almost every home to some degree. Each family is distinctively different, and each individual within a family has their own set of differences. The important thing to see is that children are being greatly influenced by what is happening in your home.

This is not intended as a judgment upon any home. I do want you to recognize that the basic quality for success in the home, the school, and the church is the quality of love. A child needs to know beyond the shadow of a doubt that they are loved. A child can respond to discipline if they know they are loved. They may not like the discipline, but love that shines through it all will help the child to withstand feelings of resistance. In the absence of real love, he has little to hold on to for support. Every child needs to be loved genuinely and continuously. Love is the greatest healing force in the whole world.

The old story about Father Flanagan's Boys Town has one brother saying to Father Flanagan after a long walk in the snow with his little brother on his back, "He ain't heavy, Father; he's my brother." Many storms come to families every day, but where true love abides that storm can be weathered.

Jesus said in Matthew 19:14-15 TLB, "Let the little children come to me, and don't prevent them. For of such is the Kingdom of Heaven. And he put his hands on their heads and blessed them." I have often said that if there is any norm for human behavior, we find it in Jesus; not that we are to be crucified as He was, but we should try to produce in ourselves the attitudes that He portrayed, obedience to the leadership of God in our lives, and recognize His Word as a guidance system.

What we see here is that Jesus loved the children. He was on a mission, he had tremendous responsibility, but he saw in little children the very Kingdom of Heaven. We are never more pure than we are as babies. Our relationship with the world is first known in our own family. As we grow older, it includes more and more relationships, but in our own family we find the shaping foundation for our future.

When we consider the future of each child, what is in our mind? Do we make a concerted effort to shape that child into a parentally conceived mold? Parents will probably make a great difference in what the child does or does not do. When a parent tries to force a child into a mold that does not fit the child, it can only produce unhappiness. On the other hand, the parent that does not assert some discipline in the development of life skills for that child may well produce failure. *Then what should be done about my child's future?* you might ask.

In answer to that question, let's consider the potentiality of an acorn. If an acorn reaches its full potential, it will be a giant oak tree, depending on what particular kind of acorn it happens to be. Some acorns can produce pin oak, some white oak, and some post oak, but their greatest potential is to fully develop into that specific kind of tree.

We need to see here that an acorn cannot possibly become a pine tree. It must develop within the bounds of its potential. I believe that every human being was created for a purpose and that they can reach the potential for which they were created. There are many factors involved for the acorn: is it used for food by a squirrel; does it fall on hard ground so that it cannot penetrate the soil and germinate; is it washed into a river and carried out to sea? Many things can happen to an acorn even as many things can happen to a child.

If an acorn falls into good soil with room to grow, given plenty of sunshine and rain, it can begin a development that eventually leads to a giant oak tree. Birds can nest in her branches when little boys are not climbing up on her limbs to build a tree house or mounting swings on her branches to provide them with pleasure. Women can plan picnics for their families and relax in her shade. Industry can come and change her form into lumber to build fine houses and beautiful furniture. Fathers can use her branches and even her trunk to provide warmth for their household in winter.

In the same way, a child with a good foundation may be used as an adult in many different ways that bring help to their fellow man. It doesn't matter as much what a child becomes; what does matter is that the child can bring forth in his life that which will produce happiness, joy, and peace. This is when a person can feel real fulfillment!

What does your child truly want to be? When given a good environment, with good communication, good family management, a feeling of love and acceptance, this child will have a very good chance for success. That's what your child deserves. If you can provide these things for your child, his or her chance of success is increased tremendously.

From a church newsletter I copied the following statement. No credit was given to an author, so I suppose its source is unknown, but it says a lot in a few words.

Children who live with criticism learn to condemn;

with hostility, to fight;

with fear, to be anxious;

with pity, to feel sorry for themselves;

Focus

with ridicule, to be shy;

with shame, to feel guilty;

with encouragement, to be confident;

with tolerance, to be tolerant of others;

with praise, to be appreciative;

with acceptance, to love;

with approval, to like themselves;

with recognition, to set goals;

with security, to have faith in themselves and in others.

How should we then live?

YOUR CHILDREN
Questions to Think About

1. As a parent, do I recognize the potential in each of my children?

2. Am I giving them enough emotional space to develop that which is being produced within them?

3. Am I nurturing their natural talents and abilities to develop them for their futures?

4. Is it possible that I am trying too hard to get them to be what I want them to be?

5. Am I emphasizing life values that will help them in their total relationship to life?

6. Whatever the present situation, what things can I do that might improve the possibilities for my children?

Focus

FOCUS ON GUILT

Years ago when I was trying to get ministers involved in the use of The Birkman Method®, I told a minister of a large church, "We like to use The Birkman Method® to give insight and other materials for inspiration, but we believe Jesus is the Answer."

To my astonishment, he said, "Jesus is the answer—to what?" He went on to say that he would not say such a thing in his pulpit, but he said, "People are always saying, 'Jesus is the Answer', but you just tell me one thing that Jesus is the Answer to."

I said, "Sir, what about the problem of guilt?"

He said, "You may have something there."

Another time I was visiting with an old doctor in a medical clinic. I am not sure how we got onto the subject, but I heard him telling me, "I am the son of a preacher, but now I am an agnostic." He went on to explain that he did not believe, if there was a God, that He was not a God of justice.

I heard myself telling him that I was inclined to agree with him. I said, "When you consider that God allowed His only begotten Son to come to earth as a baby, live a perfect life for thirty-three years, and then suffer death through a mock trial with trumped up charges and false witnesses until He was condemned to die between two thieves, and God let them get away with it. I don't see any justice in that either."

I startled him, however, when I continued, "No, it seems to me that God did not have justice for His Son, so that He could have mercy for me, through the shedding of His blood, His death, His resurrection for me."

It was just like a light being turned on in his mind. Perhaps he had come to know that he needed mercy even as I had realized even as a child that I needed the mercy of God.

We all stand before the seat of God's mercy like the old gentleman that stood before a judge. He said, "Judge, help me."

The just said, "I will try my best to give you justice."

The man replied, "But, Judge, I don't need justice; I need mercy."

The Gospel is indeed good news. In Romans 3:23-24 TLB, we read, "Yes, all have sinned; all fall short of God's glorious ideal; yet now God declares us 'not guilty' of offending Him if we trust in Jesus Christ, who in His kindness freely takes away our sins." It is true. Jesus is the answer for our guilt when we call upon Him, trust in Him, believe in Him.

A few years ago I was listening to a former New York Yankee, Bobby Richardson, as he spoke at the funeral of Mickey Mantle. Bobby told of going to the hospital along with his wife to visit Mickey. Bobby said his wife asked Mickey the question, "If you appeared at the gate of heaven, and you were asked, 'What did you do on earth to make you think that you deserve to get into heaven?' What would you answer?"

Without hesitation, Mickey Mantle answered, "For God so loved the world that He gave His only begotten Son, that whosoever believeth in Him should not perish but have everlasting life" (John 3:16).

Jesus is the answer to erase guilt from our lives. We are justified by faith in Jesus Christ. He sets us free from the bondage of sin. He gives us a new opportunity every day to open our hearts to Him and let Him come in to forgive, cleanse, heal, help, bless and make known His way unto us. He said in His Word that, "If we draw nigh unto Him, He will draw nigh unto us" (James 4:8).

After I had taken The Birkman Method® over thirty years ago, I soon began to realize that I suffered from something more than guilt. I realized that I suffered from guilt-feelings. Guilt-feelings are feelings that arise within you when you know that you are not guilty, but you feel that everyone thinks you are guilty. This type of feeling affected my life for many years. To explain fully the occurrence of this feeling, it might happen in a classroom when the teacher announces that someone took Johnny's pencil. You know that you didn't take it, but you think everyone in the classroom thinks you took it.

Another typical example of what might happen to a person bothered by guilt-feelings might be that they would not ever want to go into a store without buying something for fear that people would think they had put something in their pocket.

I still remember a song my mother used to sing when I was a small child. The words went something like this, "There's an eye watching you. There's an all-seeing eye watching you." Even though she couldn't see me, the song kept me trying to do the right thing. It probably put a holy fear in me too.

There should not be any real doubt concerning the fact that parents and other siblings can cause the growth of guilt feelings within us; for example, accusations without any degree of certainty, holding them responsible for things that happen when they do not have any means of control over a situation, or shaming them for things they do in the natural satisfaction of their own curiosity. The child begins to feel that perhaps something is terribly wrong with him. It is interesting to note that in families where this type of thing occurs, usually all of the children wind up with distorted ideas of their own guilt. When divorce occurs, many children have the feeling that they are the cause of the divorce. It takes a toll on their lives because they struggle with real guilt-feelings.

People that suffer from guilt-feelings cannot overcome it simply by being good in their own eyes. It takes an in-depth understanding of what is happening in their lives. The Birkman Method® is the best tool I have found to help people who have this problem.

The most pronounced case of this that I have seen was in a retired admiral from the Navy. He had been a submarine commander, had sunk more tonnage during World War 2 than any other submarine commander, and wrote a book entitled Overdue and Presumed Lost about the crew that he had trained. Six days after he left the command, the submarine was never heard from again. The admiral always felt guilty about the loss of the ship. How far can guilt feelings take you?

When I first met this admiral, he was retired but a patient in the psychiatric ward of a veteran's hospital. He had become an alcoholic and was receiving treatment. His wife had divorced him, and he was basically alone. I visited with him may times and saw him progress with real care and an exposure to the good news of the Gospel of Jesus Christ. He progressed so that he became a great witness with a deep impact on many people.

It looked as though the admiral was going to find his way. We moved from that city, and again he was alone. The old weaknesses began to take hold in his life. He made some bad decisions that eventually led to his death. People who have lived under the pressure of great guilt-feelings need the patient care of people surrounding them with the true compassion of Christ. Guilt-feelings are deadly without a real caring environment.

Your own feelings toward yourself can make a great difference in your life. I had been preaching for twelve years before I believed that God loved me. I didn't see how God could love me—anyone who has the kind of guilt feelings I had will probably have trouble accepting the love of God. I believed that God loved other people. I just did not believe that God loved me.

How can this translate into life? When any honor is to be given, you do not expect it because you do not believe that you deserve it. It is hard for you to believe that a person of the opposite sex could possibly be interested in you. You are always trying to be extra nice to people just so they will accept you.

Yes, even guilt feelings can produce some positive results in your life in the development of talents. You may become quite popular with people because you have to do so many nice things to buy their affection. It is painful on one hand but can be rewarding on the other.

What is important for all of us to recognize though is that God has provided forgiveness for each one of us through His only begotten Son, Jesus Christ. It is up to us to accept and receive what God has done for us.

Perhaps we all need to pray a prayer like this, "My heavenly Father, I know that I have sinned and fallen short of your glory. I ask you to forgive me and cleanse me by the shed blood of the Lord Jesus Christ. I commit myself to you to the best of my ability. I know that there will be times because of my weakness that I will fail thee, but I commit myself to keep on trying for the rest of my life to be what you want me to be. Amen."

My daughter, Ginny Baker, wrote the following poem that describes the difference a person can feel when they come to God for forgiveness. It might help you to know that she is now a minister to women in jail, co-pastor with her husband in a local church, and speaks at spiritual conferences beyond the local church. She learned enough in the brokenness of her life to be able to point the direction not only for herself, but for others as well.

WHY

You ask me why I love Jesus

And speak of Him so much—

It's all a long, long story

Of how my life was changed by His touch.

I had searched to find reality

The answers were all a sham

I wound up in a state of brokenness

And I didn't even give a damn.

Through the valley of the shadows

I tried to go at it on my own.

I found I couldn't make it—

At least, not all alone.

Then I remembered from my childhood

The story of Jesus Christ.

That He is the Son of the Living God

And for me He gave His life.

I decided to follow His Way to see

Just what would be—

And now I'll tell the whole wide world

That Jesus set me free!

Focus

"Free from what?" I guess you think
So I'll tell you just a part.
He forgave my sins, delivered me
And made me a brand new heart.
I gave him all my broken dreams and
The filthiness in my life—
He gave me joy for sorrow, and
Peace instead of strife.
So now you know why I love Him—
And why I cherish His precious name.
He is King of king and Lord of lords
And I'll never be the same.

—Ginny Alloway Baker

GUILT
Questions to Think About

1. Do I consider the importance of having my guilt resolved?

2. Do I recognize the love of God in being willing to resolve my guilt through the blood sacrifice of Jesus Christ?

3. If I am not a Christian, how is it that my guilt can be resolved?

4. Am I willing to consider the death, burial, and resurrection of Jesus Christ as an act of God on my behalf?

5. When I know that I am not guilty, am I worried with feelings of guilt?

6. Do I recognize some limitations in my life caused by guilt feelings?

7. What can I do to help my own personal esteem?

8. Do I recognize fully the differences between guilt and guilt-feelings?

Focus

FOCUS ON JUDGMENT

As Jesus is speaking in the Sermon on the Mount, He says, "Judge not, lest ye be judged" (Matt. 7:1). This sounds like an ironic statement. In *The Living Bible* it is expressed, "Don't criticize and then you won't be criticized." In a world where we need to criticize, to judge, in order to get our best performance, what can be the meaning of this particular passage? As we read further in the passage, He tells us "Others will treat you as you treat them" (v.2). Is this the core of what fights are made of—judging one another, determining without certain knowledge what someone else is thinking? Two people or two nations doing this can quickly lead to a big division.

Perhaps this is most recognizable in the home. Consider a young man and a young woman who marry. They bring into that marriage two different backgrounds of training. Each of them have set within their minds certain things that they have accepted as proper in their respective upbringing. When they marry, they soon begin to realize that all other people do not live by the same standards. They may not actually realize it, but if not, they soon find themselves arguing about some things. Some examples may be how to squeeze the toothpaste, how strong to make the coffee, the way food is prepared, and many other things. If these things become the basis of arguments, it is because of previous judgments that have already been made in regard to these things.

In a broader sense, we need to consider the emotional conflicts that can develop as two people or more interchange ideas. In marriage, these things begin to develop. At first, even though one senses a different reaction, their commitment to marriage closes the gap. As time goes on, the differences become more pronounced. Suppose one of the parties has an emotional need to be alone, and the other person has an emotional need to be with people. Without an understanding of these different emotional needs, judgment begins to take place. First, maybe they just wonder what's wrong with the other person. The predetermination of each has been set in their lives before marriage, but now it is an arena that can produce warfare, even the breakup of a marriage. One person wants to plan activities that give an opportunity to be alone. The other person is striving for activities that relate to groups in social activities. Something needs to be done to help this couple realize that their individual differences are involved. The Bible says that in marriage the two become one flesh. It does not say that there will always be agreement in that marriage. For both persons to be happy in that marriage, there needs to be room for each of them to find a way to have their inner emotional needs met. A man who likes to be alone might enjoy the solitude of hunting or fishing. A wife who needs groups could possibly become involved in a bridge club or bowling league.

If these judgments of one another are allowed to continue without understanding, where one or the other or both parties keep trying to force the other to meet their emotional need, it can be disastrous. If one person has his way at the expense of the other, it may seem all right to the person whose need is being met, but to the other it can lead to emotional distress. The happy solution is to become aware of these emotional needs and find a way for each person to have his or her emotional needs met.

A person can fast for a long time, eating no food whatsoever, only drinking water, but after so long a time, they must have food or they die. We need to realize that even though emotional needs are much more subtle, they are indeed important, and when they are denied for long periods of time, intense suffering is experienced. I need to mention, however, that surrender to the Lord Jesus Christ can help a person to endure that long-suffering.

If emotional needs have an effect in the home, they likewise have an effect in the workplace. Although people are there to work, they also have to relate to one another in most work situations. Suppose one person has an inner emotional need to talk through everything and may be so persuasive that he always wants to argue from his point of view. He may relate well to other people who enjoy this kind of banter. There may be within the workplace people who do not enjoy this type of interchange. They may live a very subjective type of life and have enough empathy toward people that they could not bring themselves to say anything that might hurt someone else.

Each one has their own set of needs, but each may look to the other with disdain. One would be saying, "What's wrong with him that he doesn't enter into our interchange of ideas and playful gossip?" The other cannot understand how anyone can be so insensitive to the feelings of other people. Both of them are comfortable in their own emotional feelings, but uncomfortable in their relationship at work. How much this interferes with their performance at work would vary greatly depending upon their responsibilities. A broader understanding of intense human emotional needs would probably help them both and reduce the stress they feel by the end of the day.

The same kind of judgments can be projected beyond the home and the job to the classroom, to the legislature, to the state department, and to all nations that are having any kind of problems. To be sure, some of these situations go far beyond personal emotional needs.

This is why we must impose the Scripture relating to judgment, "Others will treat you as you treat them" (Matt. 7:1,2). In order to resolve problems on any level, we need to treat others with respect, not that we agree with them, but that we can continually communicate until we can come to right answers in our relationships.

I heard a statement one time that said, "We sometimes have to break with people on one level in order to meet them at a higher level." Sometimes this basic attitude is employed by our state department as it relates to abuse of human rights by other nations.

Our judgments are very important to us as improper judgments can separate us from many people. So in closing this chapter, perhaps we need to judge as the old Indian saying, "Never judge another brave until you have walked in his moccasins at least two weeks." Perhaps it is best said in what is called The Golden Rule, "Do unto other as ye would have others do unto you."

JUDGMENT
Questions to Think About

1. If I have any kind of racial prejudice, can I think of people of that race that have done good things for me or the world in which I live?

2. Am I even willing to consider a different approach for judgments I have already made?

3. Would I enjoy being around a person who has the same kinds of attitudes that I have?

4. Are my attitudes providing positive results in the world in which I live?

5. Do you consider the possibility of any final judgment?

6. What positive things can I do to change negative attitudes?

FOCUS ON WORK

Galatians 6:4 says, "But let every man prove his own work, and then shall he have rejoicing in himself alone, and not in another." In *The Living Bible*, it is expressed in this way, "Let everyone be sure that he is doing his very best, for then he will have the personal satisfaction of work well done, and won't need to compare himself with someone else."

An unknown poet has expressed it in these words:

You gotta getta glory in the work you do,

A Hallelujah Chorus in the heart of you.

Paint or tell a story,

Sing or shovel coal,

But you gotta getta glory or the job lacks soul.

How many jobs really lack soul? I interpret this as meaning that a person is going through the motions of doing his job, but his heart is not in it. As much time as a person spends on the job, he really needs to have his heart in it.

An old story relates that a person stood watching as a cathedral was being built. During the day, he asked three different workers all doing the same task what they were doing.

One of them said, "I am working so that I may get paid."

The second replied, "I am working so that I can support my family."

The third one said, "I am building a cathedral to the glory of God."

All of them were working doing the same job. All of them were paid the same wages for their work, but underlying all of that, there was a difference in their attitude toward their work. Since we spend so much time on the job, how we feel about it surely makes a great difference in the amount of energy it takes to do the job.

If I go to work with a sense of dread, a feeling of terror, a lack of confidence, a negative feeling toward my job, my boss, my fellow workers, I am almost certain to have some stress through the day.

I remember a situation I spoke about previously when I was teaching school and had a different opinion than the other teachers in school. The stress became tough enough that every time I went to the teacher's lounge, I found myself praying that everything would be all right. There is no doubt in my mind that when things are not well in the workplace, it does produce great amounts of stress in our lives.

The person who feels good about what they are doing, feels competent in each task, and is surrounded by compassionate, caring people who are quick to forgive when a mistake is made is certainly a very fortunate person.

Focus on Work

You've often heard the statement, "He is like a square peg in a round hole." Interpreting that, you may be able to put the peg in the hole, but it is not going to fit snugly. There are probably a lot of people who have that kind of feeling. Can anything be done about it? Is it possible to find solutions for my problems at work?

I mentioned earlier about a man who took The Birkman Method® and started meeting with a group. It was amazing to him to discover that everyone's needs did not comply with his. Once that discovery was made, it drastically changed his treatment of those under his supervision. Relationships on the job were much better.

I thank God for The Birkman Method® and other occupational interest surveys that help people find their work in life that corresponds with their needs, their abilities, and their demand for a sense of accomplishment. When these concepts are taken into the workplace and common understandings are reached regarding their acceptance of one another and the scope of abilities of each worker, much stress can be reduced on the job. I wonder how many workers would greatly profit from that type of understanding.

When I was in seminary, it was necessary that I work to pay expenses. I was in school at Southern Methodist University in Perkins School of Theology and working at night on the assembly line for an aircraft company. I have always been the proverbial person with five thumbs on each hand. We were installing rivets, and when you made a mistake, you went to the next size rivet. I kept making mistakes until I had used the largest rivet and it would not work. I had ruined a large piece of the aircraft.

I wish to God that everyone had such a kind foreman as I had. He bought my supper at the evening break and told me how much they all thought of me. He said, "We believe that you will make a very fine minister, but we don't think your abilities as an assembly worker are very good. We encourage you to continue your ministry."

This man helped me make a decision. My physical condition had already broken down working at night and going to school for several hours a day. I had been stricken with polio a few weeks before, and upon recovery had gone back to work. The conversation with my foreman helped me to understand that I needed to be involved where my talent, ability, and desires were met—in the ministry. I dropped out of seminary, completing only two years of the required three-year course, and I accepted a full-time church position. I was much happier.

In the Bible, work originated after the incident in which the serpent deceived Eve who persuaded Adam to eat of the forbidden fruit in the Garden of Eden. In Genesis 3:17-19 TLB, God speaks to Adam and says, "Because you listened to your wife and ate the fruit when I told you not to, I have placed a curse upon the soil. All of your life you will struggle to extract a living from it. It will grow thorns and thistles for you, and you shall eat its grasses. All your life you will sweat to master it, until your dying day."

Focus on Work

Not only have men worked by the sweat of their brow, but even women who were given the pain and suffering of child birth have worked alongside men, not only doing housework and child bearing but working in fields like Ruth and Naomi. In Judges 4:4-5 TLB, we read, "Israel's leader at that time, the one who was responsible for bringing the people back to God, was Deborah, a prophetess, the wife of Lappidoth. She held court at a place now called Deborah's Palm Tree between Ramah and Bethel, in the hill country of Ephraim; and the Israelites came to her to decide their disputes." So women have served as queens, judges, farmers, realtors, merchants, and many other occupations throughout the history of the Bible. Is it any wonder that we find women, as well as men, employed in many different capacities in our modern world?

Now some good news that deals with many issues in life, but it certainly can be applied to the sanctification of our work is 1 Corinthians 15:21-28 TLB,

Death came into the world because of what one man (Adam) did, and it is because of what the other man (Christ) has done that now there is resurrection from the dead. Everyone dies because all of us are related to Adam, being members of his sinful race, and wherever there is sin, death results. But all who are related to Christ will rise again. Each however in his own turn: Christ rose first; then when Christ comes back, all His people will come alive again.

After that the end will come when He will turn the kingdom over to God the Father, having put down all enemies of every kind. For Christ will be King until He has defeated all His enemies, including the last enemy— death. This too must be defeated and ended. For the rule and authority over all things has been given to Christ by his Father; except of course, Christ does not rule over the Father Himself, who gave Him this power to rule. When Christ has finally won the battle against all His enemies, then He, the Son of God, will put Himself also under His Father's orders, so that God who has given Him the victory over everything else will be utterly supreme.

To me, the curse of work given to Adam is redeemed by the living Christ. He has overcome the source of all curses, even Satan, and all that the forces of evil represent here on earth. This simply means that I can have a work situation which is honorable both to God and men. I can fulfill the inner desire that has grown up in me to contribute to the world in which I live. I can feel good about the work that I am doing. I can get a glory in my soul for the work that I do every day. I can be at peace within myself because I know that I am doing something that is contributing to the good of mankind. Work should not be a drudgery, and it will not be when I bring even my work under subjection to the Lord Jesus Christ. Add joy to your daily life by getting your job into proper focus.

The kind of attitude you take into the work place is very

important. When you are willing to give an honest day's work for a day's pay, you are insuring your job security. It does not take too long for an employer to spot those who are drawing the pay but not doing the work. In Proverbs 6:6-8 TLB we read, "Take a lesson from the ants, you lazy fellow. Learn from their ways and be wise! For though they have no king to make them work, yet they labor hard all summer, gathering food for the winter." For people who love their work and feel that they are accomplishing something worthwhile, they have no trouble with this; but if you're only doing your job to collect your wages, you could have some trouble.

Even the wage earner should have a good attitude for earning his pay. Employers appreciate it, you feel good about it, and life becomes more pleasant.

When I taught school, there were always students in the classroom who were there for the purpose of learning. Some of the students, for any variety of reasons, were there to loaf, to distract others, to draw attention to themselves, or to just intentionally disrupt the classroom. After years of teaching, without calling attention to anyone, I would make this kind of statement; "Class, I'm sorry to say this, but we have some thieves in this classroom." That would get everyone's attention. Then I would tell them that some students in the classroom were stealing quality education time from those who were trying to study and learn. I wish I could say that it always made a difference, but it didn't. It might make a difference for awhile, but soon the same forces would be at work again. The central problem and the central answer are in each person's attitude. The person who does his job consistently, faithfully, and well is a really valuable employee. One final admonition from the Word of God supports this concept. In Proverbs 12:24 TLB it says, "Word hard and become a leader: be lazy and never succeed." "Commit your work to the Lord, then it will succeed" Proverbs 16:3 TLB talks about committing our work to the Lord. In my life, I have taught school for many years, and I have been involved in ministry all those years and many more. I have always believed that I was fully serving the Lord in each of those assignments. When you commit your work to the Lord, He will give success. I recall an incident when my wife and I had served a total of five years in a community as ministers. We reasoned that we had completed what God wanted us to do there, but we didn't know what He wanted us to do next. We knew that we could stay in that ministry and possibly be moved to another church. A missionary wanted us to come to another country and be in charge of a mission school. We considered devoting all our time to education because of the challenges and because of the need.

I was praying one morning when my wife came home from her teaching assignment for lunch. I told her that even though we had considered the previously mentioned possibilities, we had not really brought them before God in prayer. We prayed and let God know that we were willing to do any one of these tasks, we just asked God to show us clearly what to do, and we would do it. In thirty minutes, I had a phone call that provided our answer. I was sent to another church that provided the best six years and the most productive effort in all our ministry. This simply points out that God does care about you, and God is able to answer your prayer. Make Him your constant companion in all of life.

To sum this up, what should an employee do in relationship to his boss or his company? I believe that every employee needs to bring to the workplace: (1) a good attitude, (2) enough energy to give a full day's work, (3) loyalty to his boss or company, (4) a willingness to be instructed, and (5) an attitude of gratitude for the opportunity to work.

What about the boss or the company? What should an employee expect from the employer? In Proverbs 24:3 TLB we read, "Any enterprise is built by wise planning, becomes strong through common sense, and profits wonderfully by keeping abreast of the facts." There are many companies that are prospering because of those very important functions.

A company that has impressed me from its very beginning is Birkman International, formerly known as Birkman and Associates. It started out very simply: a psychologist Dr. Birkman working hard to develop his ideas. As the work expanded, he brought in other specialists and revised and improved his offerings to the business world. Then, as Microsoft™ developed Windows™, his company was there on the forefront of the business world, bringing their concepts and techniques to the whole world. This represents the very principles spoken about in Proverbs 24:3.

In Proverbs 29:2 TLB we read, "With good men in authority, the people rejoice." In the many times I have been in the office of Dr. Birkman or talked with any of the employees by phone, I have encountered happy, energetic, well-mannered people who seem to be enjoying their work experience.

Having worked as a schoolteacher and a minister for many years, I have worked under the authority of many different people. Some I have worked under have given me a good feeling of acceptance, respect for what I was doing, and genuine support in the total process. Some have given little support, little show of acceptance, and very little respect for what I was doing. You can guess which leadership I liked the best. What a difference it makes in the morale of a workplace just to have those three elements working positively toward every employee.

In Ecclesiastes 3:1-11 TLB, it says,

"There is a right time for everything:
A time to destroy;
A time to rebuild;
A time to cry;
A time to laugh;
A time to grieve;
A time to dance;
A time for scattering stones;
A time for gathering stones;
A time to hug;
A time not to hug;
A time to find;

A time to lose;

A time for keeping;

A time for throwing away;

A time to tear;

A time to repair;

A time to be quiet;

A time to speak up;

A time for loving;

A time for hating;

A time for war;

A time for peace

What does one really get from hard work? I have thought about this in connection with all the various kinds of work God has given to mankind. Everything is appropriate in its own time."

Anyone who has worked for any length of time where a number of people are involved can recognize all of these things actually happening in the workplace. (A time to kill might represent the effort to kill some vicious rumor that someone started about someone in the workplace, or to kill a project that is destined for failure.) All of these things happen in a workplace because we are all human beings. We spend much of our time in the workplace, and these things happen. It would be well for all employees to recognize this basic fact and allow for human tendencies. Certainly there are extremes that have to be dealt with individually, but for employees to be able to joke, to laugh, to develop friendships, etc., all of these things help to build positive morale in the work environment.

What does an employer owe to every employee? I think he should provide: (1) a safe workplace, safe in terms of physical and moral safety, certainly some jobs have great risks involved but pay scales should certainly include risk factors, (2) an honest day's pay for an honest day's work, (3) if possible, economically, insurance benefits for employee and family, (4) an opportunity for employees to explain themselves when mistakes are made, (5) support in the workplace to protect workers from outside intruders. These could be expanded more and more depending on the type of company that is represented. The basic element to remember is that these people are human; treat them with respect.

One final word spoken by Jesus in John 4:4, "I must work the works of Him that sent me, while it is day; the night cometh, when no man can work."

WORK
Questions to Think About

1. Do I really enjoy my work?

2. If the answer to the first question is yes, what makes it so enjoyable?

3. If I said no to the first question, what are the problems I face on the job?

4. Is my company fair to me in relationship to my job? If not, is there anything I can do to help change it?

5. Am I doing what I am supposed to do to make my company better in every way?

6. How would I describe my workplace to my wife? My friend? My boss? God? What kind of differences might there be in my descriptions?

Focus

FOCUS ON PRAYER

Many things have been said already about relationships. Most of it has been concerning our relationships with other people. Some things have been said about how we relate to ourselves. In this chapter, we are talking primarily about our relationship to God. You know what your background has taught you concerning God. Not everyone believes in God. Many who believe in God have varied ideas about who He is and what He can mean to us.

Jesus gave us the concept of God as our heavenly Father. He said that when we pray, we should say, "Our Father which art in heaven", in Matt. 6:9. In many situations the comparison we make between our earthly father and our heavenly Father would be good. In cases where people have had an abusive father, it may be a hindrance to them to think of God as a Father. Even so, the term Father would indicate a close relationship.

We must look to other words in the Scripture to help us know the character of God. In 1 John 4:8-10 we read, "He that loveth not knoweth not God; for God is love. In this was manifested the love of God toward us, because that God sent His only begotten Son into the world, that we might live through Him. Herein is love, not that we love God, but that He loved us, and sent His Son to be the propitiation for our sins." What we must recognize is that God's love is active. He knew our need for forgiveness from our sins, so he provided a sacrifice so that He could forgive the sins of all those that would come to Him. God wants to have fellowship with us, but fellowship involves more than one. If we are to have fellowship with God in prayer, we must desire that fellowship. I have often said, "Jesus is a gentleman; he does not go where He is not wanted." This is borne out in Scripture when Jesus said, "Behold I stand at the door and knock: if any man hear My voice, and open the door, I will come in to him, and will sup with him, and he with me" (Revelation 3:20).

In Isaiah 6:8, Isaiah talks about the deep spiritual experience he had with God, and he responded to God's question, "Whom shall I send, and who will go for us?" Isaiah's answer was "Here I am Lord, send me".

When the Lord told him to go and tell the people, he asked, "Lord, how long?" The answer came in the eleventh and thirteenth verses when God answered Isaiah by saying, "Not until their cities are destroyed—without a person left—and the whole country is an utter wasteland, and they are all taken away as slaves to other countries far away, and all the land of Israel lies deserted! Yet a tenth—a remnant—will survive and though Israel is invaded again and again and destroyed, yet Israel will be like a tree cut down, whose stump still lives to grow again"(TLB).

What I see in this Scripture is that God wants His loving care known throughout the whole world. Not all people will listen and hear what God is trying to say, but He will keep saying it through His prophets, His evangelists, His pastors, His teachers, His apostles, and His witnesses. He wants the whole world to know that he loves them and His messengers will always be there to tell the eternal truth—God loves you—and wants to provide an answer for your deepest needs. If you do not believe that, just give God a chance. He will help you to come to that understanding.

The other side of the Father's character is to bring all of His children unto righteousness; because the whole universe is built under a lawful system. Anyone who jumps off a ten-story building with nothing to support his weight, hoping to defy the law of gravity, does not break the law but only his body. There are many laws within the universe, and to defy any of those brings trouble to our lives. God knows that we must live in harmony with the laws of the universe in order to bring joy, peace, and happiness within. In Hebrews 12:5-7, we read, "My son, despise not the chastening of the Lord, nor faint when thou art rebuked of Him: For whom the Lord loveth He chasteneth, and scourgeth every son whom He receiveth. If ye endure chastening, God dealeth with you as with sons; for what son is he whom the father chasteneth not."

We, therefore, have the love of God being expressed to us at the same time that we are being chastened by God. The purpose of the love is to bring us to Him. The purpose of the chastening is to bring us to a proper understanding of His laws. Another part of God is His expression of mercy. You have seen a measure of it as we discussed God's love. You need to see it in terms of your interpersonal relationship with Him.

All men have sinned and have fallen short of the grace of God. That includes me and you. We both need the grace of God in this world. John Wesley, the man credited with the beginning of the United Methodist Church, was very zealous in the preaching of the gospel, having come to America to preach to the Indians. He left America, feeling that he had failed. God is the only one who can truly judge that. As he returned to England, his despair grew as a great storm arose; and he was greatly afraid, while a group of Moravians quietly and peacefully had a prayer meeting.

On his return to England, he went unwillingly to a meeting of the Moravians at Aldersgate. In that meeting, as Peter Bohler read the preface to Paul's letter to the Romans, John Wesley proclaimed that his heart was strangely warmed, and he did believe that he trusted in Christ, in Christ alone for his salvation. The Lord Jesus Christ represents mercy for all who accept Him and receive Him in their heart.

What I have spoken about is God's part in His relationship with you. You must recognize that you have a part in that relationship, too. God has made us in His own image, creatures that have power in our own will, even as God does. God does not override our will. He may seek to influence us through circumstances or witnesses, but we will never come to God outside our own will. Until we decide that we want to come to God and build a relationship with Him, we will not have any close vital relationship with Him. Even so, an old Chinese proverb states, "The journey of a thousand miles begins with the first step." Your first step in a relationship with God is to ask the Lord Jesus Christ to come into your heart.

Consider what has been said about the exercise of your will in developing a relationship with God. You use your will every day. You decide and act upon some things in your life each day that require acts of your own will. You decide what to wear. (Children under subjection to their parents may not be allowed to decide.) Adults do make their own decisions and act upon their own will in many different matters. My questions to you is, "Have you decided by your own will to develop a relationship with God?"

Like any other relationship, the more time you spend in fellowship enriches your relationship. Jesus said on one occasion, "You are my friends if you obey me", John 15:4 TLB. Again this sounds abrupt, but the reason for it is that God's laws are made to bring blessing to those who learn to obey. Much of our lives are spent trying to bring ourselves into alignment with what God wants for us.

My first prayers were honored by God as I came to Him with my whole heart. He was able to lead me into the path of righteousness. His Word, the Bible, became a lamp unto my feet, a light unto my pathway. His presence was experienced in a warmth of feeling and of peace. A hymn by Charles Gabriel states:

I stand amazed in the presence
Of Jesus the Nazarene

And wonder how He could love me,

A sinner condemned unclean

How marvelous! How wonderful!

And my soul shall ever be:

How marvelous! How wonderful!

Is my Savior's love for me.

That talks about a relationship with two good friends. One has hurt the other one but is forgiven and real compassion flows between them. That is the kind of relationship we can have with the heavenly Father through His only begotten Son, Jesus Christ.

As the relationship grows, you begin to develop spiritual eyes and spiritual ears in which you begin to see as He wants you to see and hear what He wants you to hear. A still small voice within you, not audible to your physical ears, but heard within your inner consciousness, begins to speak with you about God's direction for your life. The 16th chapter of John speaks about the Holy Spirit within you and how it works. It convicts of sin and righteousness and of judgment. Jesus is talking with the disciples about his departure from them, but He tells them that He will send the Comforter to them.

These promises are for us as well. A relationship with God brings comfort to our spirits, and peace to our souls as we learn to live in relationship with Him.

My first encounters with God brought a deep peace as I was able to submit to Him. My submission brought His comfort and eventually His power. Through difficult times, His grace has been sufficient in every time of need. When God did not grant my requests, He has been able to supply me with abundant grace to see me through every deep crisis.

After years of learning to trust God, He has given me some difficult commands. I have learned that when He speaks to my inner spirit and it complies with His Word in the Bible, it is very important for me to follow.

Fasting is a part of His Word. Isaiah 58 talks about it, and Jesus gives reference to it a number of times. I have made a facetious remark about it many times. I have said, "I believe in eating and I believe in fasting, so I just compromise and eat fast!" I guess all of us have some reluctance to fast. There are a number of ways people fast, like leaving off meat for a few days, or cutting out some things from their diet, but as far as I was concerned, I believed that fasting meant no food or beverage except water. I tried fasting a few times and fasted for as much as a week. After the first day, it seemed to be all right.

As November approached in the late seventies, I began to hear the small inner voice tell me that I needed to fast. As I inquired, and relationship involves two-way communication, I felt that God wanted me to fast for the whole month of November. As I inquired about the purpose of the fast, it was to prove to myself that I could be obedient to God. I was reluctant to begin the fast unless I was thoroughly convinced that this was God. I would turn on the television, and someone would be talking about fasting. God bombarded me with messages that He wanted me to fast.

Focus

On the first of November, I began to fast and I made this commitment. I said, "God, even if I die, I will not take anything but water through this whole month." I can tell you I had some difficulty along the way, but I was able to survive. I lost fifty five pounds, which I gained back after the fast. I had proven to myself that I could be obedient to God. I supposed God knows us well enough to know whether or not we will do what He asks us to do, but I had to know.

Since that time, I have never fasted unless God convinced me by the action of His Spirit within me. A few years later, God spoke to me in the inner voice and told me to fast beginning August 1st. I started the fast, knowing that it was for the protection of my family and my church family. On the second day of the fast, I asked God when the fast would be over. He spoke within me that it would be over at 3:00 P.M. on August 18th. I wondered about the time it would be over, but I continued fasting in obedience to the heavenly Father.

As August 18th approached, so did Hurricane Alicia. She came to the Texas Gulf Coast with a mighty blast of wind, so that even windows were blown out of skyscrapers in Houston. I was so amazed when I realized that the power of the storm had been fully spent in our hometown of Conroe, Texas by 3:00 P.M. on August 18th. It made me know that God truly knows what is happening in our world.

In my family's life, a huge pine tree growing about eighteen inches from my son's house in Channelview was blown down by the wind. It blew parallel to his house with no damage whatsoever. My other son had his truck parked next to a big pine tree. The tree broke off just above the truck and blew completely over it without touching it. One of the families in our church had twenty trees blown down in their yard, but not one of them touched their house. I am convinced that a good relationship with God is very helpful in a fragile world.

What should we say to these things—did all of this happen by chance or does God really know about the world in which we live?

A personal relationship with God is probably the most important relationship that we should develop in our lives. It is true we don't have to develop it, but God wants to develop relationship with you. He is simply waiting for you.

As you have read this chapter, some of what is written may seem very difficult and unnecessary. That is true. I was only describing my personal experience as I have developed my relationship with the heavenly Father. Your relationship with the heavenly Father will be unique as all of us are different, but each of us has the opportunity to develop a relationship with Him. For those who make the effort to establish a vital relationship with God, they shall find it greatly rewarding.

PRAYER
Questions to Think About

1. Can I accept the fact that prayer makes a lot of difference for a lot people?

2. Am I willing to develop a prayer life of my own?

3. In my expectation of prayer, is it just for what I want, or does it involve developing a relationship?

4. Is prayer primarily used in a crisis situation?

5. Does reading the Bible give assistance in developing a prayer life, particularly the Psalms?

6. What are the benefits of developing a really active prayer life?

FOCUS ON
YOUR FAULTS

In James 5:16 we are instructed, "Confess your faults one to another, that ye may be healed." Let me point out that it does not say, "Confess your sins to one another." A fault is in the problem that causes the sin, just like it is a fault in the earth that produces an earthquake. In 1 John 1:9 the Scripture instructs, "If we confess our sins, He is faithful and just to forgive us our sins, and to cleanse us from all unrighteousness." You will notice that He is capitalized, showing that we confess our sins unto God who cleanses. Thus, we assume the difference between confessing faults and confessing sins. Faults we confess to one another; sins we confess unto God who forgives.

As we spoke of faults that produce earthquakes, we are speaking of the geological layers of the earth that do not come together properly. It may not be visible on the surface, but where these faults occur, the earth can suddenly shift and an earthquake occurs. That is a very simple explanation of major things that happen on the earth. When an earthquake happens, a lot of people may be injured by the results.

The same thing is true if our faults are ignored and we do not get help to overcome the faults in our human personality. This is why James instructs us to confess our faults one to another that we may be healed.

I think our faults, in a spiritual sense, develop when our thoughts and actions are contrary to the Word of God. We are then in opposition to the Word of God, and without correction it can be a deadly destructive force in our lives. We may try to cloak our faults and deceive ourselves into thinking that our behavior is acceptable, but we only break ourselves in the process of deception. We need to face up to the facts regarding our faults. We need to take a personal inventory of what we are doing and see if anything is contrary to what the Scripture teaches. A few good questions might be:

1. In my life, am I keeping the Ten Commandments?
2. Do I have the attitudes Jesus expressed in
    Matthew 5:1-12?

If you get that far and don't find any problem, then remember Jesus' conversation with the rich young ruler. (Luke 18:18-29.) Jesus told him to keep the commandments. When he answered that he had done that from his youth on up and asked what did he yet lack, Jesus said to him that if he wanted to be perfect, he needed to sell all that he had and give it to the poor and then follow Him. In his case, he turned away sorrowfully. He could not pass the test, at least, not for that moment. Some sources indicate that he may have overcome his reluctance at a later date and became a devout follower of Jesus.

In any case, it seemed possessions were the seat of the problem. Years ago I attended a spiritual retreat. At that time,

Focus on Your Faults

I was young enough to meet with the youth. A young lady had inherited millions of dollars and the story of the rich young ruler led her to believe that she should give away all of her wealth and follow Jesus. Dr. John Biegeleisen of Eden Theological Seminary told her that she had already passed the test. She was willing to give up everything for Jesus. He told her that what she should do is follow Jesus and be a good steward of that which she possessed, making it available to Him as He directed her in her spirit. She didn't have the fault the rich young ruler found within himself.

There is an old story about three preachers from the same town who went to a distant convention and were lodging together. After much talk, one of them suggested that they confess their faults to one another. He went on to say that when he got out of town, he loved to gamble. The second stated that when he got away from his home town, he loved to go to a tavern and drink sometimes until he was drunk. There was a long pause as they looked at the third preacher wondering what he would disclose about himself. Finally he said, "Fellows my secret fault is gossip, and I can't wait to get back to town." We have different kinds of faults, but if we are going to be healed, we have to come to the point where we can confess those faults to others in order to be healed.

In our society, we have many types of support groups. Perhaps the most noteworthy is Alcoholics Anonymous that reaches into many communities in our world. As each one addresses the group, he gives them his first name and then says, "I am an alcoholic" and continues by telling how long he has been able to go without a drink. They know that the healing process cannot begin as long as a person denies that he is an alcoholic. In any support group, acknowledgement of the problem is vital for the help that is needed. Anyone who is a Christian ought to be able to make this acknowledgment, "I am a sinner, but I confess that Jesus Christ is my Savior because I have accepted His death for my redemption, the shedding of His blood for the remission of my sins, and His resurrection from the dead in the flesh as my victory over Satan and all evil forces in this world." The church is not made up of perfect people. It is made up of people who commit sins and are dependent upon Jesus Christ for their salvation. Even as doctors practice medicine and sometimes make mistakes, in the church we are practicing Christians, and we need support, not only from Jesus Christ, but from others as well. The church should be a great support group.

In a former book, *It All Began in Slate Valley*, I talked about a parolee from prison who was totally adjusted in his community, except that he was afraid to go to church, because he was afraid of being rejected. Just because a person has made mistakes in their life, they should not be rejected by the body of Christ. In the story of the prodigal son, the prodigal came back willing to be a hired servant in his father's house. He did not come to dictate to the father, but only to be a servant. Any special-interest group seeking to infiltrate the church with the purpose of advocating beliefs contrary to the word of God should indeed learn from the attitude of the prodigal son.

Where does a fault originate? In many cases the germination of faults comes in early childhood. Anyone who steals may have grown up in an environment where stealing was acceptable; the only thing wrong with it was getting caught. Someone who is very deceptive may have learned as a child that if they lied, they could get out of trouble. Someone who cheats other people might have learned in school that their grades were better when they copied someone else's homework. An alcoholic may be repeating what he saw in a mother or father. There are endless possibilities for the germination of thoughts that produce faults.

One case study that I am familiar with and use by permission is the study of a professional man that had sexual problems. In the early development of his life, he became sexually active. He lived in a community where there was much promiscuity between boys and girls. Boys had the mistaken idea that it was all right for young boys and girls to have sexual intercourse. This man disclosed that he had sexual relationships with girls before he was old enough to attend school. In his mind it was all right to have sex.

As he approached his teen years, he not only continued his pursuit of sexual relationships with girls, but was also seduced into a sexual relationship with a married woman who had befriended him. A pattern of promiscuous relationships was well developed by the time he was an adult.

In his professional career, even though he fought against the inner nature that had developed, there were times when he was overcome by his fault.

He went to a psychiatrist in recognition of his problem. This was the beginning of his healing. Even as the Scripture states,

"Confess your faults one to another that you may be healed." This beginning was important in turning around from a fault deeply imbedded in a person's subconscious nature.

Through The Birkman Method® and working through his problem both in individual counseling and in support groups, he was able to come to grips with his issues. He came very near to some human earthquakes, but his faith in the Lord Jesus Christ brought him through to victory. He is now living a victorious life because he recognized his fault and confessed it to others who helped him through the darkness and into the light.

People in our society are recognizing the need for support in dealing with their faults and the people that are affected by them. In our small city of Conroe, Texas, which has grown tremendously in the last thirty years, we have a real-life example. Back then, the church dealt with most problem situations, but now there are a number of support groups meeting. Listed in a recent paper in this small town, we have these groups:

1. Alcoholics Anonymous
2. Al-Anon support group for Alcoholics Anonymous families
3. HIV support group for HIV positives and their families
4. AIDS care support group
5. Take off Pounds Sensibly
6. Mended Hearts—Cardiology patients and their families
7. Overeaters Anonymous
8. Caregiver support groups (for people who care for spouses, or shut-ins)

9. Parents' support—for families dealing with unacceptable behavior

Add to these several similar groups not listed, and you can see that people are recognizing their need for help with critical problems of every sort.

Having worked with The Birkman Method®, a questionnaire that helps people focus on their personality, I believe that a person profits greatly in the disclosure of faults in their inner nature to a trusted group. I have worked with a number of groups that have developed real compassion for one another as they struggled through some deep crisis. I have seen stress greatly reduced, people breaking through prison bars of their own making, not allowing their talents to spring forth. People who have lived in relative isolation have become vital contributors to their church and community. I think every person can truly profit from being a part of a group that develops real communication in their lives.

In 1965, I went through one of the most meaningful experiences in my life in CAUSE 11, which means Counselor Aides University Summer Education. It was a government program. We had lectures every day, but then we met with the same group every day for four hours in what they called "group dynamics." It was THAT, all right. We talked about anything and everything about each one in the group. We told the group anything they wanted to know and the things that we thought were important . Our leaders were skilled in helping us to break through into real communication which sometimes involved crying, laughing, and many other emotions.

It helped me the most by helping me to realize that I could face up to myself. We need to get out of our darkness and into His (God's) marvelous light.

It is true that in some churches, Sunday School classes develop into real support groups. Prayer groups, when people communicate with one another as well as bringing their petitions before God, may become support groups that meet deep emotional needs. Other types of meetings could develop what is needed.

Dr. Roger Birkman, himself the son of a Lutheran minister and the originator of The Birkman Method® has been interested not only in his business but also in making his materials available to churches to strengthen the church. His own church, First United Methodist Church in Houston, Texas, has used it. Other churches throughout the country have used it. I have used it in every church I have pastored for the past thirty three years and find it to be greatly helpful in developing meaningful support groups. I highly recommend the use of his materials to help people face up to themselves and learn to properly relate to God, themselves, and others.

I recently completed a group with people from the same church. The following statements are excerpts from their written analyses of the group:

> "Every time I went to a meeting, it pertained to what I was going through at the time. The group helped me to make it through the trials and circumstances I was walking through. It gave me a new understanding and insight on how to pray better according to my personality."

"My 15-year-old daughter and I gained real help in our understanding as the needs and strengths were discussed. We realized how our different components fit together. It helped me realize a lot of emotional responses that we all have in certain situations and why we handle them the way we do. This has been an eye-opening experience to me, and I highly recommend it for everyone. It was very uplifting, and I am continually seeing benefits from it."

My husband and me: "We were both impressed by the scope and accuracy in The Birkman Method® in delineating our personality profiles. It really seemed to be substantially 'on target.'"

"I began participation in The Birkman Method®, not knowing what to expect. My husband and I learned a great deal about our relationship because it defined our similarities and differences, portrayed our personalities, and highlighted our talents. Some things I had been seeing as detriments were actually viewed as talents in the Birkman analysis. The group dynamics helped us to know not only ourselves better but to understand and appreciate one another's giftings."

"The Bible states that we should "love our neighbor as ourself." But if you do not love who you are first, you cannot and will not love your neighbor. The Birkman group helped me to see myself as God created me and to be content in that. Each one of us has different talents, and by discovering those talents and incorporating them in to the body of Christ, true unity will come!"

"The Birkman evaluations we received provided an invaluable tool for understanding the differences in personalities that drive the dynamics of our day-to-day interactions. Not only did they help me understand myself better, they provided insight which helped me to understand how my personality affects others, as well as the needs that others may bring to the table when interacting with me. Combining this with the understanding of the Holy Spirit and the dynamics of group interaction, the Birkman study group I participated in gave me insight and information that I will be able to draw upon for years to come."

YOUR FAULTS
Questions to Think About

1. What is the difference between sins and faults?

2. Am I aware of any faults in my own life?

3. Is there some support group in my community that can help me to overcome this fault?

4. Is there a Sunday school class or prayer group in my church that might be a support group for my need?

5. Is my fault serious enough that I might need intensive counseling? An example might be a treatment center for drug use.

6. How could my life improve if I can overcome this fault?

7. Would I be interested in forming a support group using The Birkman Method®?

Focus

FOCUS ON JESUS

I t all started in prayer therapy...

On the evening of February 8, 1962, I went to my first prayer therapy meeting at the St. John's Methodist parsonage in Port Acres with Rev. Henry Alloway in charge of the meetings.

I want to say right here that that first meeting was the turning point in my life. When Henry Alloway began the meeting by saying, "Let's just picture Jesus as standing in the center of the room." Then He turned and looked at each one of us and said a few words. Then when He turned and looked at me, I just melted. Jesus was so real at the moment I could have reached out and touched Him. It seemed to me that Jesus looked right into my heart, and I wanted to change.

After that I began to read and study my Bible, and I read *Prayer Can Change Your Life*. I also started praying regularly each night and morning as soon as I awoke.

On the night of February 19, 1962, as I was praying, I came to a decision. I decided I wanted to turn my life over to Jesus. I did just that. I surrendered everything that I was. It was a <u>TOTAL</u>, unconditional surrender—I didn't leave anything out. When I said, "Jesus take my heart and cleanse it and give it back to me so that it will be a fit place for thy Holy Spirit to dwell," that's when it happened. My heart just swelled and got so big it nearly jumped out of my chest—then it just opened up and God's love poured into my heart. Then wave after wave of love flooded over me. Waves of warmth went over me and through me and into my heart. I knew without a doubt that God had heard me, and He forgave me for my sins. My heart felt as light as a feather, and I felt wonderful and completely different and changed from then on. The Holy Spirit seemed to hover around me for weeks after that, and I was walking on a cloud.

I was a chain cigarette smoker at this time. I smoked at least two packages a day. Something (a small voice inside) kept after me to give up smoking. Finally on the night of March 12, I told Jesus that I was giving up cigarettes for Him—to show Him that I really had surrendered <u>everything</u>. I promised Him that I would never smoke another cigarette. I asked Him to help me and to strengthen me and take away the desire for cigarettes. For the next two or three days, I went through <u>hell</u> fighting the tobacco habit. With God's help, I conquered the tobacco habit. Thank God! I had smoked for thirty years.

On Sunday night March 18, 1962, (the first night of our revival) I re-dedicated my life to God. I had already surrendered in my heart, but I just couldn't resist going up to the altar. I wanted to do something for Jesus. The next night of the revival, March 19, after I got home and prayed to God before I went to sleep, I was just quietly lying there, when the Holy Spirit began to move on my lips. I got up and went into the dining room and got on my knees and yielded to the Spirit. I began to speak in a tongue I didn't understand. I don't know how long I stayed on my knees, but when I got up, I realized I had received the baptism of the Holy Spirit. I was so happy and at peace with myself.

I guess I just realized in the beginning that like the book *Prayer Can Change Your Life* by William Parker and Elaine St. John said "What gets your attention, gets you") and Jesus got my attention the first time I went to prayer therapy.

This is what prayer therapy has done for me.

Anita Davidson

This statement of one person's experience when they set their focus on Jesus has been duplicated many times over in the hearts and lives of believers.

The story has been told about a missionary who went to a poverty-stricken area of the world where people had very little to eat. She gave a full glass of milk to a little boy, and the little boy looked up into her eyes and asked the question, "How deep shall I drink?"

This seems to be the question a lot of people are asking when they consider their relationship with the Lord Jesus Christ, "How deep shall I drink?"

I can go to church and maintain a pretty good relationship with God and not be considered a fanatic by anyone. What kind of response would the boy have had if the missionary had replied, "Take just enough so that everyone can see that you've had a drink."

Others become involved in the work of the church and receive blessings from God as they reach out to others. In giving, they receive blessings from God. They may know that they are serving God, but may not be satisfied fully in their relationship with the Lord.

Focus on Jesus

I remember preaching a sermon one time on the text, "Not every one that saith unto me Lord, Lord, shall enter into the kingdom of heaven; but he that doeth the will of my Father which is in Heaven" (Matthew 7:21).

When I completed the sermon, I called on my Sunday school superintendent to pray. He couldn't speak but wept openly before the people. Later he told me about the fact that God had called him to preach, but he didn't think he could do that so he compromised the issue by working hard in the church. It did not satisfy his need. He entered the ministry and hundreds, if not thousands, were lead to Christ through his ministry.

What if the missionary had said to the boy, "Just drink enough to satisfy your thirst, but do not drink to satisfy the need of your whole body." The boy would have had a good taste but a longing for more would still have been there. I would not be surprised if many people find themselves in that same situation.

Besides the Scripture given already, the price of disobedience to God is very costly. In 1 Chronicles 10:13-14, "So Saul died for his transgression against the Lord, even against the word of the Lord, which he kept not, and also for asking counsel of one that had a familiar spirit, to inquire of it; and inquired no of the Lord; therefore he slew him and turned the kingdom unto David, the son of Jesse."

When Jesus initiated the Lord's Supper, the Scripture says in Matthew 26:27, "And he took the cup and gave thanks, and gave it to them, saying 'Drink ye all of it.'" This may have a double meaning; first that he wants everyone to drink of the blood of the new covenant, Jesus Christ. Secondly, he wants us to be totally involved in God's purpose for our lives.

In Mark 10:35-40, this story is told:

And James and John, the sons of Zebedee, came unto him saying, Master, we would that thou shouldest do for us whatsoever we shall desire. And he said unto them, What would ye that I should do for you? They said unto him, grant unto us that we may sit one on thy right hand, and the other on thy left hand, in thy glory. But Jesus said unto them, Ye know not what ye ask: Can ye drink of the cup that I drink of? and be baptized with the baptism that I am baptized with? And they said unto him, We can. And Jesus said unto them, Ye shall indeed drink of the cup that I drink of; and with the baptism that I am baptized withal shall ye be baptized: But to sit on my right hand and on my left hand is not mine to give; but it shall be given to them for whom it is prepared.

This indicates that God gives this glory to those who drink all of the cup, who give themselves unto complete obedience unto what God gives them of His instructions.

Dwight L. Moody was in his mid-twenties teaching Sunday school. He wondered what would happen if a person would give his whole life in obedience to God. He gave his life to God to see what would happen. Millions of people were touched by Moody's life.

Whatever is left of your life, God can use it to bring great blessing in this world and give you His glory in heaven. Keep your focus on Jesus. If you ask Him, "How much shall I drink?" He will answer, "Drink ye all of it."

JESUS
Questions to Think About

1. Am I willing to consider, "Who is Jesus?"

2. Am I willing to read the gospels Matthew, Mark, Luke and John as though I had never heard of Jesus?

3. Am I willing to examine my prior beliefs about Jesus and give Him a chance to relate to me?

4. In Revelation 3:20 Jesus says, "Behold, I stand at the door, and knock: if any man hear my voice, and open the door, I will come in to him, and will sup with him, and he with me." Am I willing to ask Jesus to come into my heart?

5. How deeply will I drink in terms of my personal relationship with Jesus?

FOCUS ON
STEWARDSHIP

In the 25th chapter of Matthew you can find the parable Jesus used to help people understand what God expects of them. It is the parable of the talents. In the parable Jesus is teaching us that each of us are given talents. He is also teaching us that those who use their talent wisely will be given even more. As a matter of judgment, He is saying if we don't use it, we lose it. He is trying to motivate us to use what we have and see the growth in our life.

What is a man's talent? In the parable He is using money as the standard of measurement. Does this mean that we will be judged by the balance in our checkbook? From that parable alone you might be correct except for what he says in the rest of the chapter. Before that parable in verses 1-13 He gives a parable about the ten virgins. They were expecting the bridegroom, but only half of them were wise enough to take extra oil for their lamps. As the five foolish virgins rushed out to get oil before the bridegroom came, they were too late, the door was shut, and they could not gain entrance. I believe that the bridegroom means Jesus, and that man must make responsible decisions regarding the only begotten Son of God, Jesus Christ. I believe that our heavenly Father is saying through Scripture that He will not tolerate the rejection of Jesus Christ.

A lot of people rejected Jesus when He was walking as a human being on earth. I believe that when Jesus cried out of the cross, "Father, forgive them; for they know not what they do" (Luke 23:34), He was talking not only about the soldiers who crucified Him but everyone who had rejected Him. I believe that He wants every human being to come into the fold of God, but He knew, as we know by the Word of God, that there is a day of judgment. He wanted all people to pass this first test.

It was true in His generation, and it is still true in our generation, that not everyone will open their heart to ask the Lord Jesus Christ to come into their heart and life. They may be waiting for the bridegroom, but they are foolish in their lack of preparation. We need to search our hearts and see what is keeping us from embracing with our faith the Lord Jesus Christ.

In the case of the high priests in Jesus' day, they had such strong doctrines in their mind that had descended through their heritage that they could not accept him. There are many doctrines in our world today that men uphold so strongly that it keeps them from developing a vital personal relationship with the living Lord, Jesus Christ. If you know that you are living just outside that close vital relationship with Christ, you need to change it today. You need to pray a prayer like this: "Lord Jesus Christ, I do believe that You are the only begotten Son of God. I do believe that You suffered death upon the cross for my salvation. I believe that Your blood was shed on the cross for the forgiveness of my sins. Lord, I have committed many sins, but I ask You to forgive me, to cleanse me, to restore me to a right relationship with You. I do ask You, Lord, to come into my heart and help me to follow You, Amen." Then you might read Romans 10:1-10 in your Bible, also John 3:1-21, and Revelation 3:20-22 "Behold, I stand at the door and knock: If any man hear My voice, and open the door, I will come in to him, and will sup with him, and he with Me. To him that overcometh will I grant to sit with Me in My throne, even as I also overcame, and am set down with My Father in His throne. He that hath an ear, let him hear what the Spirit saith unto the churches."

The climaxing sentence here is, "He that hath an ear, let him hear what the Spirit saith unto the churches." In theological circles there has been a lot of teaching and discussion about human beings regarding their body, mind, and spirit; or it may be spoken in terms of outer man (the body), the inner man (the soul or psyche), and the inner most man (the spirit). It is in the spirit that man truly connects with God.

In John 3:5-6, "Jesus answered, verily, verily, I say unto thee, except a man be born of water and of the Spirit, he cannot enter into the kingdom of God. That which is born of the flesh is flesh; and that which is born of the Spirit is spirit." You will notice the difference here in the capitalization, or lack of it, in the word spirit. When speaking of God's Spirit, it is in capital letters; and otherwise it is in small letters.

What keeps a person from coming into a vital relationship with God in his spirit? God welcomes everyone who comes humbly and asks Jesus to come into his heart. John Wesley's father, even on his deathbed, spoke to John Wesley about the inner witness. John Wesley described his encounter at Aldersgate, "I felt that I did trust in Christ, in Christ alone for my salvation." That is the inner witness when a person opens their total being unto the Lord Jesus Christ and asks Him to come in. There is an inner witness in the spirit that causes him to know that he is born again of the Spirit. In the stewardship of life, every person needs to make that connection with the Spirit of God.

I spoke earlier of the high priests whose hearts were so hardened by an inner doctrine that they could not accept Jesus as the Messiah, the Anointed One. They missed the great opportunity they had and were not even able to recognize it. So much for them, many people in our modern world are missing it too.

In the prophecies of the Old Testament, how can people read these and not accept the fact that they were spoken about Jesus? I call your attention to Isaiah 9:1-7 and Isaiah 53:1-12. One is talking about His birth, the other His death. One might also read all of Psalms 22. I ask this question: "Is there any other man, besides Jesus of Nazareth, that has fulfilled these prophecies?" Is it possible that your doctrines in your soul or psyche have kept you from coming into a vital relationship with the Lord Jesus Christ? It is the stewardship of your life in the balance. In the last judgment, according to Jesus' parable of the ten virgins, some will go in, and for others the door will be shut. The invitation has been given to come. Now is the time to be a responsible steward of your own life. God has made a way for you through His only begotten Son, Jesus Christ.

Focus on Stewardship

When Jesus gave the parable of the talents, it represented money for those people. We all need to have the proper respect for money. It is not to be worshiped, but rather used in subjection to almighty God. Jesus gave good advice in Matthew 6:19-21, "Lay not up for yourselves treasures upon earth, where moth and rust corrupt, and where thieves break through and steal: But lay up for yourselves in heaven, where neither moth nor rust doth corrupt, and where thieves do not break through nor steal: For where your treasure is, there will your heart be also."

What do you do with your money? In Malachi 3:8-12 we read,

> *Will a man rob God? Yet ye have robbed me. But ye say, wherein have we robbed thee? In tithes and offerings. Ye are cursed with a curse: for ye have robbed me, even this whole nation. Bring ye all the tithes into the storehouse, that there may be meat in mine house, and prove me now herewith, saith the Lord of Hosts, if I will not open you the windows of heaven, and pour you out a blessing, that there shall not be room enough to receive it. And I will rebuke the devourer for your sakes, and he shall not destroy the fruits of your ground; neither shall your vine cast her fruit before the time in the field, saith the Lord of Hosts. And all nations shall call you blessed: for ye shall be a delightsome land, saith the Lord of Hosts.*

A story is told about a woman with great possessions from all around the world. She kept them and adored them, decorating her beautiful country home with them. One day a friend was visiting and admired a beautiful ivory elephant from India. The hostess gave the ivory elephant to her visitor. A few weeks later, the friend learned that the woman who had given her the elephant was away from home, and the house burned to the ground with all her lovely possessions. The friend took the ivory elephant and went to the burned out house. She found the lady who owned it in tears. She embraced her and then gave her back the ivory elephant, and the woman said, "Isn't it strange, the only thing I have left is what I have given away."

Where is your treasure? Do you greedily hoard your possessions, or have you put them, too, under the lordship of Jesus? Any person with money has the responsibility of good stewardship with it.

There are other kinds of talents too. In the use of The Birkman Method®, we have seen that each of us has a set of emotional talents. To give you an example of what I am talking about, the component pages of The Birkman Method® show an interpersonal need. When the emotional need is being met, corresponding talents begin to develop. For instance, a person who needs a sense of orderliness in their life develops a talent for finding a place for everything and keeping everything in its place. This person would be valuable in filing information, and they would always have a clean, orderly desk. They would also feel very uncomfortable in a situation that could not be brought into an orderly system.

Focus on Stewardship

Each of us has a set of emotional needs that help us develop particular talents in our lives. The person who has a great need for acceptance may become quite friendly and do all kinds of things for other people just because of their own inner need. When our talent, whatever it is, has been committed to Jesus, then it can be profitable in the kingdom of God.

Dr. Birkman committed his talent to Christ and wanted to share it with others. He was one of the original founders of Talent-Sharing, Inc., a non-profit corporation developed to help people commit their talent to Christ and share it with others.

The greatest example we have had thus far was a widowed teacher, Della Gussie Easterly. As sixty-five she retired from the Crockett Texas Independent School District. She then went to south Texas and taught where teachers were greatly needed. At seventy-two, with diagnosed heart trouble, she went to Jamaica and taught for ten years in a mission school, not accepting any salary but living on her retirement.

The man who founded the school was Rev. Ben Swett, an alcoholic who found Jesus to be sufficient for his needs. He was a gifted singer and gave his talent to the Lord. While ministering to death row inmates in a Jamaican prison, he gave all twelve of them a New Testament and found out that only one of them could read. This man, with a great voice, read to the other eleven men. That is when Ben Swett decided to build a school in the hills of Jamaica not far from Mandeville. God used that school tremendously. Ben Swett was able to be with the man who read to the other eleven on the morning of his execution. They read the nineteenth chapter of Job. The condemned man's great voice rang through the prison yard on his way to the gallows; they could hear him singing at the top of his voice, "Lord, I'm coming home."

Just how far can a talent dedicated to the Lord Jesus Christ reach? It reaches all the way to heaven for those it has touched in the name of the Lord Jesus Christ.

What does God expect of you? It is written right there in Matthew 25:35-36,

> *For I was an hungered, and ye gave me meat; I was thirsty, and ye gave me drink; I was a stranger, and ye took me in: Naked, and ye clothed me: I was sick, and ye visited me: I was in prison, and ye came to me."*

Then the righteous spoke saying they didn't remember doing these things for the King–but He answered, "Inasmuch as ye have done it unto one of the least of these my brethren, ye have done it unto me." Matthew 25:40.

STEWARDSHIP
Questions to Think About

1. Have I made adequate preparation to meet the bridegroom, Jesus Christ?

2. Am I responsible for the use of my talents?

3. What is my attitude toward my possessions? Who will they belong to in 100 years?

4. Do I recognize any areas of need in this world where I can lend a helping hand?

5. I everyone in the world had the same attitude that I have about helping others, what would happen in our world?

6. What on earth are you doing for heaven's sake?

Focus

FOCUS ON
THANKSGIVING

As we try to develop a correct interpersonal relationship in a three-dimensional way: God, self, and others; it is very important that we learn to give thanks. Have you ever known of anyone who was offended because someone thanked them for what they had done? They may not have been looking for thanks, perhaps they viewed it just as something they should have done. Still, the giving of thanks probably made them feel a little better in their spirit.

I suppose this might be what happens when we begin giving thanks unto God. The giving of thanks unto God may cause the Lord to feel so good in His Spirit that He just wants to return the blessing unto us. I know that when I begin to give thanks unto God for all that He has done for me, I soon begin to feel much better in my spirit.

In the book of Psalms it says, "Enter into His gates with thanksgiving, and into His courts with praise: be thankful unto Him and bless His name" (100:4). In Psalms 95:12 we read, "Let us come before His presence with thanksgiving, and make a joyful noise unto Him with psalms." All through the Psalms you find references regarding thanksgiving and praise unto God.

Focus

In Psalms 103:1-5 it is like the psalmist is preaching to himself, reminding himself that he needs to give constant blessing and praise unto God, for He says,

Bless the Lord, O my soul; and all that is within me, bless His holy name. Bless the Lord, O my soul, and forget not all His benefits: Who forgiveth all thine iniquities; who healeth all thy diseases; who redeemeth thy life from destruction; who crowneth thee with lovingkindness and tender mercies; who satisfieth thy mouth with good things; so that they youth is renewed like the eagles."

Sometimes I have to preach that sermon to myself when my spirit begins to be depressed and I can't seem to find my way out of my dilemma. Then to begin thanking God for all that He has done, is doing, and will do for me, I soon begin to feel better, think better, and I see the crisis pass.

When you couple the Scriptures above with the one found in Psalms 22:3, "But Thou art holy, O Thou that inhabitest the praises of Israel", you learn that God lives in the praises of His people. The word *inhabit* means to "live in or dwell in." If God then lives in the praises that come forth from our hearts unto Him, we do not have to push our imagination very far to reason that as we praise God we become more and more conscious of His presence with us. People who experience this regularly, the praising of the Lord, bear witness to the value of praising God.

A number of years ago now, I read a book by Merlin Carothers entitled, *Prison to Praise.* In this book he was talking about praising God at all times, no matter what the situation. As people praised God, things turned around, and blessings followed. When I first read the book, I had a very negative response to it, but the second time I read it, I thought it was perhaps the most helpful book I had ever read.

Perhaps you wonder how you can give thanks in everything; perhaps you wonder how you can praise God in some of the circumstances in which you find yourself. Let me share an experience with you that might be helpful.

From 1973 to 1979, I was pastor of St. Paul's United Methodist Church in Conroe, Texas. In those years I had added to my staff a very devout minister by the name of Jim Carroll. Jim was a saintly person, and his wife Henrietta was equally so.

In June of 1979, I was moving to another church, so Jim resigned to take another position that he was offered. The first week in the new position, he and his wife attended a prayer meeting. On their way home, their car was struck by a train and dragged down the tracks. Jim and Henrietta both survived the wreck, but Henrietta died a few days later.

Jim lay for months in Herman Hospital in Houston. I visited him often. One day Jim, who always seemed to minister to me, gave me a lesson I will never forget. He said, "Henry, you know the Scripture found in 1 Thessalonians 5:18, 'In everything give thanks; for this is the will of God in Christ Jesus concerning you.' He said, "I have been having trouble with this Scripture; how could I give thanks for that accident and the death of my wife and the horrible injuries I have suffered?"

I waited while Jim continued. "Then, the Lord showed me that it was not FOR everything we give thanks, but the Scripture says IN everything give thanks." He continued, "I can do that!"

Jim did continuously give thanks through all of his health problems. He lived to be a pastor again, to be married again, and to minister to many people. Jim learned to give thanks IN everything.

I am not ashamed of the gospel of Jesus Christ; I have seen it bearing forth such great results in so many people.

The story is told of a great evangelist Hugh Price Hughes who was challenged to a debate by an atheist Charles Bradlaw. As Hughes had the right to set part of the rules of the debate, he answered that he would meet Bradlaw at the designated place but that he would bring with him 100 witnesses that would tell about how Jesus Christ had saved them from terribly degrading lives as adulterers, drunks, thieves, and other kinds of sin. Hughes then asked Bradlaw to bring with him 100 witnesses that could tell personal stories of how much atheism had helped their lives. Charles Bradlaw did not show up for their debate.

You are the one who knows how your life has been. You know whether peace and joy are a part of what you feel regularly. If peace and joy are missing, it may be that you have been seeking them in the wrong way. God does not condemn you, He wants to help you. Try giving thanks and keep on doing it until you begin to feel a change take place within you. Remember, the Lord inhabits the praises of His people.

In your relationship with people, you might remember the time in the Scripture when Jesus healed the ten lepers. (Luke

17:11-19.) The focal point of the story is that when the ten lepers were cleansed, one of them came back and gave thanks unto Jesus. In the seventeenth verse, "And Jesus answering said, 'Were there not ten cleansed? But where are the other nine?'" We need to give thanks to the people that contribute so much to our lives.

Just as an example for you, I want you to know that I give thanks unto many, many people who have had so much to do with the development of my life. Let me just enumerate some of them to help you realize how much thanks we need to give:

1. My wife of fifty-eight years, Virginia, a great companion

2. My parents who loved me and taught me values

3. My grandparents whose influence was so great

4. My children, who have taught me far more than I have taught them, and the beautiful people they married

5. Our grandchildren, both in my bloodline and those whom we consider a part of our family. Each one has contributed greatly to our joy

6. Our great-grandchildren, a delight to all of us

7. My brothers and my sister for all the wonderful things they have done and their great spouses who add to all our lives

8. My first-grade teacher and all the other teachers that have contributed to my life

9. Teacher colleagues that have been great teammates

10. Bosses that have guided me to better workmanship

11. Christian laymen in every church I have ever served who have been used by God to richly bless us

12. All of the good neighbors we have had and the ones we have now

13. Special thanks to Dr. Birkman for the insight he has shared

I have mentioned these things to help you realize how many people really deserve the thanks you could give them. But there is one more group that I would like to thank, especially for the joy they brought to my life. These are the children I have taught in twenty-three years of teaching in the public schools of Texas. Each one has added blessing to my life.

One group especially, in my last year of teaching prior to retirement, blessed my life abundantly. They were all sixth-graders. The principal, Cathy Cornwall, gave us permission to enter educational drama contests in southeast Texas. We did not have any speech or drama classes, so the kids had to work after school and whatever time they could find to work at school. We attended three festivals, and kids receiving a superior rating in any event qualified to enter that same event at the State Festival in Beaumont, Texas. We had thirty-nine children that qualified. The odds were against us at the State Festival because all we had were sixth graders. The other schools had speech classes and

Focus on Thanksgiving

sixth, seventh, and eighth grade students all competing at the same level. When the final tally was given, this group of students had won third place at the State Festival. I need to thank them for their splendid effort, their great spirit of cooperation, and their great response to coaching.

When we stop long enough to think about all the people that have been so important to all of us in our lives, we would have to include such people as doctors, nurses, bankers, mechanics, garbage collectors, salespersons, and yes, even lawyers. The list could go on and on.

What about myself? I probably need to be thankful for all of the good decisions that I have made that resulted not only in a blessing to me but to others as well. I give thanks for the times I have been submissive to the Lord so that He could use me as a vessel in His hands.

Don't be too hard on yourself. You've made many good decisions. You've done many good things that are worthy of thanksgiving. Lighten up, love yourself even as you love others. Your thanks in three dimensions will add life to your years.

THANKSGIVING
Questions to Think About

1. How do I feel when someone says "thank you" to me?

2. Do I suppose that the feeling I receive would in some way be duplicated in others when I say thanks?

3. When the Scripture says, "The Lord inhabitest the praises of His people," what is it talking about?

4. Have I ever spent some quality time just giving thanks unto God?

5. If not, would I be willing to experiment with giving thanks, to see if it really helps in my life?

6. Have I ever been thankful for myself because I knew that I willfully did the right thing?

FOCUS ON LIGHT

When Jesus said, "Ye are the light of the world" (Matthew 5:14), He was making a statement about what he expects of people who follow Him. Maybe we need to think about what light really means in a world that has so much darkness.

What does light do? It destroys darkness. It provides vision—a much clearer, more certain perspective. When refracted by a prism, it produces much color. Light is also used to provide warmth. Light travels faster than sound. As a laser beam, it is used in surgical procedures or to illuminate performances of rock and roll musicians. Light is used in many different ways to help mankind. With all of that, does it answer what Jesus was talking about?

I believe that Jesus was talking about an inner source of light that would illuminate the countenance of a person. This light would sparkle with joy. This light would show the serenity of peace. This light would radiate warmth to other people. The light that Jesus radiates through His followers does provide surgery in the soul of a man through a word fitly spoken. The anointing of God in a person's life causes great illumination and enhances their performance in all of life.

Focus

Jesus said further in Matthew 5:14-16,

A city that is set on a hill cannot be hid. Neither do men light a candle and put it under a bushel, but on a candlestick; and it giveth light to all that are in the house. Let your light so shine before men, that they may see your good works, and glorify your Father which is in heaven.

In that sense, Jesus is looking to us to be the light bulbs, the laser beams of this world. Even as a light bulb needs a source of power to be that light, a Christian needs the power of the Lord Jesus Christ to maintain that light in a world with much darkness.

One thing that we have talked about through the years as we have conducted group meetings on The Birkman Method® and in our preaching is what causes the light to go out. We know in our knowledge of a common light bulb that sometimes a short occurs in the circuit and the light goes out. Sometimes a major outage of power produces darkness over a whole city. The source of the short or outage has to be found to have the light restored.

Unfortunately, that can happen to Christians too. They can have their light snuffed out when the power source stops. If that is true, and it is, what causes the power outage? What can be done about it?

At the outset of this book, the theme was providing a means to develop an interpersonal relationship with God, self, and others. You may not realize it, but God expects us to maintain a good relationship with Him; but included in that relationship is a good attitude toward ourselves and others.

In Matthew 5:21-24, Jesus says,

Ye have heard that it was said by them of old time, Thou shalt not kill; and whosoever shall kill will be in danger of the judgment, But I say unto you that whosoever is angry with his brother without a cause shall be in danger of the judgment. And whosoever shall say to his brother Raca (idiot) shall be in danger of the council; but whosoever shall say, Thou fool shall be in danger of hell fire. Therefore, if thou bring they gift to the altar, and there rememberest that they brother hath aught against thee; leave there thy gift before the altar and go thy way; first be reconciled to thy brother, and then come and offer thy gift.

God deals in reality. He wants us to relate to Him in a real sense, and He wants us to relate to our fellow men in a real sense. How many people realize that their lights have been short-circuited because they are too proud to go and apologize to someone they have offended? You may think that it doesn't amount to much, but it does according to Jesus' teaching in the Sermon on the Mount.

I remember a sad situation in a former ministry. Two men had fallen out of fellowship with one another over something that had happened between them. The one who did the wrong thing never went to apologize and try to renew their friendship. The other would not even try to forgive the other man, even though I talked with him at length about forgiveness. Their disagreement meant more to them than the Lord Jesus Christ. Their lights went out and gave way to bitterness that grew up in their souls and kept their spirits from shining through to light up their countenances and their lives.

Anytime you are unable to forgive your fellow man, you are shorting the circuit of God's power in your life. God's power does not flow through unforgiveness. In His Word, He even says, "If you won't forgive, He won't forgive you" (Matthew 6:9-15). Forgive your fellow men and let your light shine.

You may wonder how you can forgive someone who has hurt you, but you can. I remember, quite vividly, a woman who was hurt terribly by a wealthy, powerful man. This man had told lies about her husband, who was a minister, that hurt her terribly. She suffered a cerebral hemorrhage that she attributed to the pressure this produced. How could she forgive this man? She struggled with it intensely until finally the Lord showed her this man as a baby. He was pure and happy and healthy. He had been corrupted by the world in which he lived. He did not heed Jesus' warning that we must be in the world but not of the world. Yes, sometimes it is difficult to forgive, but we must do it for our light to shine.

Jesus wants us to actively pursue good relationships in our lives. In the Scripture quoted from the Sermon on the Mount, Matthew 5:21-24, Jesus says that if we remember that anyone has aught against us, we are to go and make it right. We are to actively pursue right relationships with everyone in our lives. That is not always an easy challenge, but if you are serious about letting your light shine in a dark world, it is a matter of necessity.

We sometimes use an illustration about triangular neon light. If one side represented God, one side self, and the remaining side others, we could have a beautiful light as long as the power was operational. Just short that power on any one of the three sides, and the whole light goes out. We need a good relationship with God. We need a good relationship with ourselves, and we need a good relationship with others.

Jesus told us to let our light shine. I am in control of the light of my life and you are in control of the light of your life. We do not have to make the effort to let our light shine, but think about the consequences. We are like a man reading a newspaper in the light. The light goes out and he is still trying to read the newspaper. The light makes a great difference in our lives and the lives of other people. Our effort to let the light shine will be rewarded. God knows where the light shines; and if it is not shining, He knows what is wrong and what you need to do to get the power source fixed. Check in with God and let Him lead you to the place where your power needs to be fixed. Let Him tell you what to do to make the necessary repairs. God is with you. He never leaves you or forsakes you. If you are real with Him, He will be real with you.

LIGHT
Questions to Think About

1. Do I understand the meaning of the exercise of my will in turning light on or off in relationship to God, other people, and myself?

2. What do I enjoy most, light or darkness?

3. What is my attitude toward other people? Does it change rapidly when relating to some people?

4. What can I do to make any darkness in my life become light?

5. In the creation story, the Bible says that God said, "Let there be light and there was light." This was a willful act on God's part, and light was produced. If I will to bring light with my life, what do I expect will happen?

FOCUS ON LOVE

Wˣhen a lawyer asked Jesus the question, "Master, which is the great commandment in the law?" (Matthew 22:35-36), Jesus answered (Matthew 22:37-40),

> *"Thou shalt love the Lord thy God with all thy heart, and with all thy soul, and will all thy mind. This is the first and great commandment. And the second is like unto it. Thou shalt love they neighbor as thyself. On these two commandments hang all the law and the prophets."*

If all the law and the prophets hang on these two commandments, they must have vital importance in our lives. How does a man love God? How does a man love his neighbor? How does a man love himself? These three questions need to be answered if we are to fulfill what God has intended for our lives.

When we think of God, we must have some kind of conception. When I was a child I pictured God as an old man with long white hair and a long white beard who looked down on all the earth. I believed that He had a huge book and my name was on one of its pages. I believed that there were two columns, one showing marks for the good things I had done and other with marks for each evil thing I had done. I felt that the evil side was far heavier than the good side. I was afraid of the God of whom I had pictured in my mind.

I was so glad when I heard the story of Jesus and found that He had suffered death on the cross for me, that His blood had been shed for the remission of my sins, and that if I would accept Him as my personal Savior, I would be cleansed of my sin. I accepted Him, and I can still remember how clean I felt.

The Scripture tells us that no one comes to the Father but by Him (John 4:6). To truly know God, we accept His only begotten Son, Jesus Christ. I recognize that this may be very difficult for some people whose ideas have grown up in a faith that does not accept Jesus, but it is done every day all across the world as people come to know God through His only begotten Son. I had the privilege of leading an elderly Chinese man and wife to the Lord Jesus Christ. They were Buddhists and could not speak English, but as their son interpreted for them, I told them about Jesus, they accepted Him, and they were born again into the kingdom of God. They are now in heaven according to the promise of God the Father.

Accepting Christ is one thing, living for God on a day-by-day basis is something else. How does a man show his love for God? In Mathew 25:35-40, we have shared already about the King in Jesus' parable that truly represented God. In this parable, he said, "I was hungry and you fed me, naked and you clothed me, thirsty and you gave me a drink, I was sick and in prison

and you came to me." The righteous then answered that they
didn't remember doing those things for Him. He then answered,
"Inasmuch as ye have done it unto one of the least of these my
brothers, ye have done it unto me."

I believe that man's love for God is very active. He may
not be aware that what he is doing is really for God, he just
sees a need and rightfully does what he can to help in that
situation. How many times have I've seen people's love for God
transformed into acts of kindness toward their fellow men?

For some people, their real problem relates to loving
themselves. It is true that the Scripture tell us to deny ourselves
and take up our cross and follow Jesus. This is nothing wrong
with that, but some people stop with just denying themselves.
They may treat themselves slanderously, speak bad things about
themselves, not allow themselves any pleasure, always treating
themselves with disdain. When the Scripture says that we
should love our neighbor as ourself and we treat ourself with
such cruelty, what benefit could our neighbor expect from us?

Through the use of The Birkman Method®, I learned a great
deal about myself. One of the things that I learned about me
was not only that I didn't truly love myself, but I really didn't
like much about me. With that frame of mind, it was difficult to
look for much success. I would work hard and do many things
for people just trying to be accepted. It was my own attitude
toward myself that was wrong. God truly wants us to recognize
that we are creations of God and that we have a purpose in this
life that only we can fulfill. We need to be able to press forward
to fulfill that for which we were created.

Focus

The apostle Paul had many talents. He expected to succeed. He believed in himself and his ideas strongly enough that he was out to persecute anyone who believed differently. Then Paul was greatly changed in an encounter with Jesus on the Damascus road and recognized that in himself he was not good. He said in Romans 7:24-25: "Oh wretched man that I am! Who shall deliver me from this body of death? I thank God through Jesus Christ our Lord. So then with the mind I myself serve the law of God; but with the flesh the law of sin."

We need to think well of ourselves, but we need to follow the heeding of the Scripture, not to think more highly of ourselves than we ought. The one factor that can help us to think properly of ourselves is a personal relationship with Jesus Christ.

In John 15:1-14, Jesus says,

I am the true vine, and my Father is the Husbandman. Every branch in me that beareth not fruit he taketh away; and every branch that beareth fruit, he purgeth it, that it may bring forth more fruit. Now ye are clean through the word which I have spoken unto you. Abide in me, and I in you. As the branch cannot bear fruit of itself, except it abide in the vine; no more can ye, except ye abide in me. I am the vine, ye are the branches; he that abideth in me, and I in him, the same bringeth forth much fruit: for without me ye can do nothing. If a man abide not in me, he is cast forth as a branch, and is withered; and men gather them, and cast them into the fire, and they are burned. If ye abide in me, and my words abide in you, ye shall ask what ye will, and it shall be done unto you. Herein is my Father glorified that ye bear much fruit; so shall ye be my disciples. As the Father hath loved me, so have I loved you: Continue ye in my love. If ye keep my commandments, ye shall abide in my love; even as I have kept my Father's commandments, and abide in His love. These things have I spoken unto you, that my joy might remain in you, and that your joy may be full. This is my commandment, that ye love one another, as I have loved you. Greater love hath no man than this, that a man lay down his life for his friends. Ye are my friends, if ye do whatsoever I command you.

I cannot force myself to love properly. Love is the product of giving my life to Jesus Christ, letting His life come forth in me. When we abide in Christ and trust in Him for leadership; when we accept His Word in the Bible, when we translate his Word into action through our faith, then love supernaturally grows into maturity in our hearts.

Jesus leads us to accept ourselves. In accepting the lordship of Jesus Christ, a person can quit striving to keep up with everyone else. He can put himself to the task of becoming what God has created him to be. What a disappointment it would be to strive all of your life and then find that all of your striving was only good in this world. You could not turn it in at the gate of heaven and make yourself acceptable unto God. Words will not provide for us entrance into heaven apart from the saving grace of the Lord Jesus Christ. We need to make sure that we do not get the cart ahead of the horse, so to speak. Put Jesus Christ first in your life and He can help you solve all of your dilemmas about life and death and eternal life. Jesus is the King of kings and the Lord of lords.

I have seen so many people changed by His love when they allowed Him entrance into their hearts. I remember a man who was fifty-six years old. He had never married and he was what the community thought of as a hopeless drunk. He would have ended his life that way, except for Jesus, and his final willingness to let Jesus Christ come into his heart and his life. He met Jesus when his body was broken. He was walking across a major highway between two beer joints one night. He saw the car lights approaching, but he saw two sets of headlights and didn't know which way to go. He was hit by a car. In that broken state, he was able to accept Jesus. He never drank again, but he became a servant to all. He truly loved people and they loved him. He was about ninety years old when he died.

One of the greatest compliments I ever received came from a man I met at his brother's funeral. This man was in a wheelchair, his body twisted with disease. I went to visit him many times. He did not want to talk about Christ, but he did allow me to pray for him before I left. After some time, he was in the hospital and was gravely ill. I went to see him and was greatly shocked when he said, "I do not believe in Jesus, but I believe in you."

I spoke to him with words given in that instant by the Holy Spirit. I said, "I want you to know that the reason I come to see you is because I love you. The reason I love you is because Jesus has put that love in my heart."

He then said, "In that case, I believe in Jesus." He accepted Jesus as his personal Savior and lived a happier life the rest of his days. This only demonstrates that Jesus loves you no matter what your attitude has been toward Him. You can have a living, vital relationship with Him, if you'll ask Him to come into your heart and life.

How do you love others? A lot of people try to force themselves to love others by the force of their own will. It doesn't work any better than pulling yourself up by your own bootstraps. Love is generated from within; it springs up like living water from its true source, Jesus Christ. In fact, when you give yourself in obedience and faith to Jesus Christ, along with love growing inside you, you will see joy, peace, patience, kindness, goodness, faith, meekness, and self-control. These are all the fruits that grow in us when we abide in the true vine, Jesus Christ, for these are all a part of His character.

In Tolstoy's story, "Where Love Is," the theme is, "Where love is, there is God." An old man is looking for the master Jesus Christ to come that day. He is trying so hard to get his home cleaned up to welcome the master, but he keeps having interruptions, people with real needs. He just keeps having to leave to help them, and then the day is over and he is sad because he missed the Master. Then the word came to him that the Master had come disguised in each of the opportunities he was given. Indeed, he had met the Master.

In the book of James we are told, "Faith without works is dead" (James 2:20). He goes on to say that Abraham was justified by works when he offered up his son Isaac on the altar. Our faith in Christ is what produces the good works in God's sight. In 1 Samuel 15:22 we read, "Hath the Lord as great delight in burnt offerings and sacrifices, as in obeying the voice of the Lord? Behold, to obey is better than sacrifice, and to hearken than the fat of rams."

Anyone who has not learned to obey the voice of the Lord and follow through with faith has missed some very great experiences with God.

Several years ago, about 9:00 A.M. I was in my study praying. We lived in Conroe, Texas. As I prayed, the inner voice of the Spirit of God spoke to me and said I was to be in Kingston, Jamaica by 6:00 P.M. that evening. This startled me because I had been to Jamaica several times, and the plane out of Houston at 8:30 A.M. was the one that made the proper connections. I was just going to dismiss the thought, but it kept recurring quite strongly within me. I knew that there was going to be a banquet given by a group of Christian businessmen there that night in honor of Prime Minister Seago. I had been with the group that had gone down to set up the banquet. In my natural mind, I realized the impossibility of it. I had no money, no credit card to use for airfare, and knew of no plane connection. I said to God, "If this is really You talking with me, I can do it. If it is not You, it couldn't work out anyway, but I'm going to do all I can to get there." I called a friend with a travel agency to try to find a way. I called my son-in-law and got permission to use his credit card. I called the treasurer of my church and asked for one hundred dollars to use for the weekend. Everything worked out, and I was in Kingston, Jamaica by 6:00 P.M. that evening. I knew it had to be God, because when I got to the airport and went directly to the boarding area, they were already boarding. My name was called over the loudspeaker to report to the boarding desk. They told me that another passenger wanted my seat to Miami because it was next to her friend. Then they asked me if I would mind sitting in the first-class section!

God confirmed the reason for my being there. I attended the prime minister's banquet that night. The next night another banquet was held to try to bring a Christian men's organization there. My three-minute witness made a difference. Men responded and a Christian business men's organization was developed. God can do big things. He always has, He always will. Your obedience in faith will be the greatest adventure in your life.

So, what about love? It is active. You are always looking forward to opportunities that will not only become the spice of your life, but they will bring great blessing to others and to the shaping of God's eternal kingdom. Abide in Christ and let His Word abide in you. The fruit of love will grow into maturity.

LOVE
Questions to Think About

1. If I were to be tested by God on my love for God, self, and others, what would my grade be on a scale of 1 to 100?

2. Do I give any importance to the need for love to be generated in my life?

3. Can I love people properly purely from the generation of my own will?

4. Is there anyone, including myself, that I am having trouble loving?

5. When Jesus says, "I am the vine, ye are the branches," He is talking about life coming through Him to the branches. Am I willing to let His life flow through me?

6. Do I need a change in the quality of love in my life?

FOCUS ON
ETERNAL LIFE

It is nearly 9:00 A.M. Sunday morning. I am almost ready to leave for church. The phone rings. A man has been shot!

Any minister can relate to unexpected news about tragedy. In this case it was a thirty-five year-old man who was the father of five children from 9 to 16 years of age. I flew with the wife, her brother, and her husband's sister to the distant state where the man had been shot. He was shot by a man on drugs who came up to the car in which the man was riding and shot him in the temple. He lived for four hours after our arrival. These people needed some answers that would really make sense. Their grief had to be dealt with in a way that their hearts could be comforted.

In a different situation, what would a minister say when called to a funeral home to minister to family members whose father has taken his own life? Dependence upon the leadership of the Holy Spirit and the Word of God is essential. When I had to deal with this, I was thankful that God could give some instant instructions for this family. I told them first that this was not done with a sound mind. His emotional turmoil had become so great that he did not think he could deal with it.

Rather than seek help, he chose suicide. I told them that they needed to repudiate this act in recognition that their father had made the wrong choice. If they didn't do this, they would be bothered by the thought that this was what to do in the face of great problems. They had one thing their father did not have and this was the knowledge of how much this kind of thing hurts the family. I welcomed them to come and talk with me any time they had a problem.

What are we to think about suicide? Some people have different thoughts about people who commit suicide, but God judges all of us, and I am thankful that Jesus said in John 5:25, "Verily, verily, I say unto you, the hour is coming, and now is, when the dead shall hear the voice of the Son of God: and they that hear shall live."

In over forty years of ministry, I have conducted many funerals. Some have been infants, children, adolescents, young adults, middle aged adults, and older adults. It doesn't matter what age people die. It seems that for their loved ones and their friends there is always a need for the question to be answered: "If a man die, shall he live again?"

I believe the Scripture emphatically states the answer to that question. I would like to share with you what God has shown me.

The first evidence I would give you regards David, a man in Old Testament history who was very real in his relationships to life. At times his possessions overcame him, and he allowed sin to come into his life. He tried to cloak it so that casual observers would not notice, but David knew, and God knew about his sin.

He had sent a soldier to the front, believing that he would be killed, and he was killed. David's purpose was to have that man's wife. He was guilty before God but tried to deceive himself into believing that he was all right. God sent Nathan the prophet to bring Him to his senses. You can read this story in the Bible in 2 Samuel 11 and 12.

You can also read about David's repentance in Psalm 51. He wrote seventy-three of the Psalms. He is said to have been a man after the Lord's own heart. He strived for obedience but sometimes failed, but he never quit trying to follow God, to do what God wanted of him.

David's most famous Psalm was the twenty-third Psalm. Having lived hundreds of years before Christ came to the earth as the baby Jesus of Nazareth, David still had faith in life beyond the grave. He speaks of his faith is Psalms 23:4-6,

Yea, though I walk through the valley of the shadow of death, I will fear no evil: for Thou art with me; thy rod and thy staff they comfort me. Thou preparest a table before me in the presence of my enemies: Thou anointest my head with oil; my cup runneth over. Surely goodness and mercy shall follow me all the days of my life; and I will dwell in the house of the Lord forever.

He expected to be with the Lord for all eternity. He had faith in the everlasting kingdom of God.

Focus

When Jesus came to earth as a baby and lived thirty-three years before going to the cross, He trained disciples and gave many teachings and was an example before mankind. He knew that death was imminent for Him, so He called His disciples together and talked with them about His death and what would happen. In John 14:1-4 Jesus says,

> *Let not your heart be troubled; ye believe in God, believe also in me. In my Father's house are many mansions: If it were not so, I would have told you. I go to prepare a place for you. And if I go to prepare a place for you, I will come again, and receive you unto myself; that where I am, there ye may be also. And whither I go ye know, and the way ye know.*

This has been the hope and trust of Christians ever since Jesus died, was raised from the dead on the third day, ascended into heaven, and sits at the right hand of God the Father. Our faith is in Him for everlasting life. But some may ask, "How can this be for us?"

The apostle Paul lived in the same generation as Jesus, but the only way he could know Him was through faith in his own heart. We have to become acquainted with Christ in our hearts by faith. Paul didn't believe until the Lord came to him as a blinding light, but when he asked, "Who are you, Lord?" a voice answered, "I am Jesus whom you persecute." From that moment, Paul had faith in the Lord Jesus Christ.

Focus on Eternal Life

In 1 Corinthians 15, Paul gives his faith in the resurrection of Christ. I call your attention to a few of those verses, "Now if Christ be preached, that He rose from the dead, how say some among you that there is no resurrection of the dead? But if there is no resurrection of the dead, then is Christ not risen, And if Christ be not risen, then is our preaching vain, and your faith is also vain" (vv. 12-14). Then in verses 19-22,

If in this life only we have hope in Christ, we are all men most miserable. But now is Christ risen from the dead, and become the firstfruits of them that slept. For since by man came death, by man came also the resurrection of the dead. For as in Adam all die, even so in Christ shall all be made alive.

He climaxes this teaching in the verses 55-57 of this same chapter. "O death, where is thy sting? O grave, where is thy victory? The sting of death is sin; and the strength of sin is in the law. But thanks be to God, which giveth us the victory through our Lord Jesus Christ." And then His personal word to you in verse fifty-six, "Therefore, my beloved brethren, be ye steadfast, unmovable, always abounding in the works of the Lord, forasmuch as ye know that your labor is not in vain in the Lord."

Life is everlasting. We shall continue our life somewhere. Jesus Christ is the answer for those who want to spend their eternity in heaven with the only begotten Son of God, Jesus Christ.

Focus

If you do not know Him, you may wonder about spending eternity with Him. Get to know Him here on earth, and then you will rejoice over being with Him for all eternity. Remember, He is available to you now. He cares about you. He will help you here on earth and make death a triumphant experience, if you, by faith, will ask Jesus to come into your heart and life.

ETERNAL LIFE
Questions to Think About

1. What personal experiences have I had with death?

2. Have I found the help I have needed to overcome my grief?

3. If I have lingering problems, is there a support group, perhaps in my church, that can help me?

4. What do I suppose would happen to me if someone I love died instantly?

5. Do I recognize in the Bible the fact that men have faced death triumphantly?

6. Would it be a wise thing to find answers that would help me face death victoriously?

Focus

FOCUS ON FAITH

The kinds of choices you make every day represent your faith. You choose what you believe is right for you. It not only makes a difference then, but it makes a difference regarding your future choices as well. Young people between the ages of 15 and 22 make some of the most important choices of their lives. Between those ages many of them choose what kind of a job they want, who they want as a mate, and other complex choices regarding friends, attitudes, and basic philosophies. They may not even realize the importance of their will in making these choices, but whatever they choose, it will make a great difference in their lives.

Joshua recognized the importance of the human will in making choices. Thousands of years ago he made this statement found in Joshua 24:15,

And if it seem evil unto you to serve the Lord, choose you this day whom you will serve; whether the gods which your fathers served that were on the other side of the flood, or the gods of the Amorites, in whose land ye dwell; but as for me and my house, we will serve the Lord.

Focus

Parents need to realize the impact their choices make for their children. I am so glad that my dad made the same choice Joshua made, "As for me and my house, we will serve the Lord." I was nine years old when my dad made that choice, and we all went to church together, and every member of my family committed their lives to Christ. It made a difference for all of us. We began enjoying a rich life of fellowship with other Christians and with the Lord Jesus Christ. The preacher would come and stay with us on occasion. Other families would visit, and together we enjoyed gatherings around the piano. As my sister played the piano, we sang hymns of praise unto God. That is what we were doing on December 7, 1941, when a neighbor came and told us of the Japanese attack on Pearl Harbor. My dad's choice made a real difference for all of us.

Think about the choices you are making every day. Do any of them reflect the development of an individual relationship with Almighty God? Do you pray daily, allowing time for meditation so that God might guide your thoughts? Do you read the Bible and let the spirit of God lead you to what you need to think about that day? Do you spend any time in thanksgiving for what God has done for you? Do you praise Him with all of your heart? Are you willing to do whatever you think He wants you to do? If your answers to all of those questions is no, then you know that you are not allowing God much time in your life.

If you cannot say yes to most of the questions above, then you need to determine what choices are most important to you. You might ask yourself some questions like: *Am I using my choices for the sole purpose of building up my wealth on earth? Am*

I so consumed with my job that I spend almost my total strength and ability in pursuit of success in my job? Am I such a social person that I am constantly seeking friends and contacts to improve my social life? Perhaps the question you need to ask above all else is this: *Are my choices leading me to God or away from Him?* Your life is involved in all the choices you make.

Dr. Peter Marshall, when he was chaplain of the United States Senate, was called on to preach at the Naval Academy in Annapolis, Maryland. He had a prepared message, but as he waited to speak, the Holy Spirit prompted him to speak on an entirely different text. It was James 4:14, "For what is your life? It is even a vapor, that appeareth for a little while and then vanisheth away." Many of those young men soon entered the service and gave their lives for their country. The morning he spoke was December 7, 1941.

The truth is that none of us know the future, but we do know that the choices we are making today shape our future.

Paul said, "I can do all things through Christ who strengthens me" (Philippians 4:13). God wants you to fulfill the purpose of your life. God can't do it Himself; He needs the cooperation of your will. When working together with God, you have a great chance of becoming more than you ever thought you could be. Your choices make all the difference.

In Hebrews 11, and I recommend that you read this faith chapter in the Bible, in the first verse I quote The Living Bible, "What is faith? It is the confident assurance that something we want is going to happen. It is the certainty that what we hope for is waiting for us, even though we cannot see it up ahead." We do not have to know what the future holds, but we can know Who holds our future when we commit our lives unto the Lord Jesus Christ.

In closing this book, I want you to know that God really cares for you. I don't care what you have done or are doing. I know that God stands behind His Word to perform it. He can and will accept you as you are, and He will help you to add real life to your living, and He has already prepared for you a place in heaven through His only begotten Son, Jesus Christ the Lord.

One time I heard a story about a young man who won a college scholarship in football, but he never was more than a third teamer. He was very close to his father, and often his father would come to the campus to visit him. They would walk arm in arm, across the campus. As the boy was nearing the close of his senior season, he had played only sparingly. Then the final game came, and he asked the coach to let him play. The coach reluctantly put him in the game, but the boy played with such fervor and success he couldn't remove him from the game. He was the player most responsible for the team winning the game. When the game was over, the coach called him aside and said, "Son, what happened today? You were great!"

The boy said, "Coach, did you ever meet my father?"

The coach replied, "I saw the two of you walking across the campus together, but I never did meet him. Besides, what does that have to do with how you played?"

The boy said, "Coach, my father was blind; he never got to see me play football, but this week, he died. He is now in heaven, and this was the first game he ever saw me play."

Does that sound fantastic? Maybe it is, maybe it isn't, but if you took time to read all of the eleventh chapter of Hebrews, the faith chapter, you'd be glad to know that the very next verse of Scripture is very exciting. In Hebrews 12:1 TLB says,

Since we have such a huge crowd of men of faith watching us from the grandstands, let us strip off anything that slows us down or holds us back, and especially those sins that wrap themselves so tightly around our feet and trip us up; and let us run with patience the particular race that God has set before us.

Whatever you are doing, they are plenty of people who care about you. Most of them are here on earth, but remember that life is everlasting and some of them are in heaven. God bless you all!

FAITH
Questions to Think About

1. I have faith in some things. What are they?

2. Do I know that as I launch my life into the future, the direction that I point my life will make a great difference in what happens?

3. What do I want to happen in my life for the future?

4. My faith in the present frames the picture of what will happen in my future life. What do I expect to happen?

5. A lot of people are looking at me, whether I realize it or not. Does that make any difference to me?

6. I cannot live my life over, but I can begin today making all things better than they have ever been. What do I want to do about it?

FOCUS ON
SALVATION

To give you a little background on the cover, the picture is an original painting by a young artist whose name was Donald Devers. Don was a member of a church we pastored in Port Arthur, Texas. While he was visiting relatives in Houston, Texas, he attended a meeting where I was preaching. As I was giving the invitation, the Lord prompted me to say, "The Lord showed me that there is someone here that has never been saved. If they will come to the altar tonight, they will be saved."

I could hardly believe what happened. There must have been at least 100 people who responded and many tarried until about 11:00 p.m. The Lord spoke again in my spirit and said "The one I was talking to you about has not come."

I looked to my left and saw Don Devers talking with two men. When he saw that I was free, he came to me and said, "I wanted to be saved but these men told me that I could not be saved until I knew the Bible." I told him that was not true, that all he needed to do was to repent of his sins and ask Jesus to come into his heart. When I said that, he threw himself on the altar and wept about fifteen minutes. When he rose, he turned to the man behind him and said, "When I knelt down, I hated you but God has changed all of that to love."

About a year after Jesus became the Lord of his life, Donald died in a fatal car accident. In the short time period after he was saved and before he died, Donald talked to almost everyone he came in contact with about his relationship with Jesus, and painted some original pictures of Jesus as he saw him in his heart. It is clear to me that God was able to use him mightily in the time Donald had left on the earth.

He is survived by his wife Mary Jo and his son Keith. His wife gave permission for this picture to be used.

PRAYER OF SALVATION

God loves you—no matter who you are, no matter what your past. God loves you so much that He gave His one and only begotten Son for you. The Bible tells us that "...whoever believes in him shall not perish but have eternal life" (John 3:16 NIV). Jesus laid down His life and rose again so that we could spend eternity with Him in heaven and experience His absolute best on earth. If you would like to receive Jesus into your life, say the following prayer out loud and mean it from your heart.

Heavenly Father, I come to You admitting that I am a sinner. Right now, I choose to turn away from sin, and I ask You to cleanse me of all unrighteousness. I believe that Your Son, Jesus, died on the cross to take away my sins. I also believe that He rose again from the dead so that I might be forgiven of my sins and made righteous through faith in Him. I call upon the name of Jesus Christ to be the Savior and Lord of my life. Jesus, I choose to follow You and ask that You fill me with the power of the Holy Spirit. I declare that right now I am a child of God. I am free from sin and full of the righteousness of God. I am saved in Jesus' name. Amen.

If you prayed this prayer to receive Jesus Christ as your Savior for the first time, please contact us on the Web at **www.harrisonhouse.com** to receive a free book.

Or you may write to us at

Harrison House • P.O. Box 35035 • Tulsa, Oklahoma 74153

ABOUT THE AUTHOR

Dr. Henry O. Alloway, PhD. is an author, retired Methodist minister, former teacher, coach, and radio announcer. He spent 23 years teaching in Texas Public Schools at the junior high and high school levels. He also coached basketball, baseball, speech and drama events. Along with all of this, he served as a radio announcer in football and basketball and announced one State Championship in football. He served as a Methodist Minister for many years and now assists his son-in-law at the Church of the Saviour in Conroe, Texas.

Dr. Alloway earned his PhD. in Christian Philosophy from Homestead College of Bible in Orlando, Florida. He has been married to his wife Virginia for 59 years. Together they have 3 children, 9 grandchildren and 16 great-grand children.

Contact Dr. Alloway at:

1912 Ed Kharbat Dr.
Conroe, TX 77301

936-756-1113

www.cotsconroe.org